© Carla McCloskey 2015
FIRST EDITION

ISBN 978-0-578-16271-3

Background Cover Art from
Codex Tor by Leigh J. McCloskey

For information on this and other works visit
www.leighjmccloskey.com

Grandma Told Me So

Lessons in Life and Love

Carla McCloskey

This Book Is

Dedicated to My Dear Wise Grandmother

Mary V. Steele

July 12, 1892 – November 13, 1979

You Are With Me Always

Pip Pip, Ducky!

Contents

Grandma Told Me So

Lessons in Life and Love

Foreword

I am honored that my beloved Carla asked me to write the forward for her exquisite and meaningful book, *Grandma Told Me So*. Carla's unconditional and wisely conditional love has healed my heart and set my soul free to say yes to the adventure of being human, of raising a family together and opening the remarkable journey of being a father and husband. My relationship with her and our children is a fount of joy and the most meaningful part of my earthly sojourn.

Carla has been and remains my teacher who gives me advice worth heeding, my muse who inspires me to ask better questions, my true friend who tells it to me like it is. Because of her powerful honesty and insights, I have learned to trust her judgment and intuition with increasing admiration over the years. I know I can rely on her sense of things and her motivation in saying them, which is, I believe, why we experience true partnership together.

I am delighted that Carla has put down in words her wisdom, humor and pragmatic balance between the demands of living life, the desires of the heart and the yearnings of the soul. I have always admired Carla's love and respect for her Grandma's special knowing and guidance that has been so important to her. Her Grandma set a tone—a pure and beautiful note of humanity—like a jewel in Carla's heart. Grandma's teachings are a radiance of good will and optimism, a love of simple things and honest living with integrity and balance.

Carla reminds us, as does her Grandma, to approach life with gusto and curiosity, but to do so with generosity, worthiness and laughter.

Life, love and relationship are our greatest human art forms and lifelong works in progress. By entering into the mystery of relationship and the responsibilities of true love, we cultivate our hearts and grow a garden of possibility together. After all, we are sharing this world together.

— Leigh J. McCloskey

Prologue

BEING A BETTER YOU

For years people have told my husband and me that we are an inspiration to them, that knowing us makes them believe a great relationship is possible. They often ask us for advice. People love to talk about their problems or complain about their relationships, but it's difficult for them to do the work and make the changes in their lives you might suggest to them. Why? Because you can never tell people what to do. They must discover it themselves.

The best thing you can do for anyone is to be a good example. As my dear Grandmother would say, "Walk what you talk," Maxim #18. My grandmother had dozens of these sayings that generally summed things up quite well, a shorthand for those people with few words, but wise hearts. Many of these sayings we have all heard before, some may have been my grandmother's own invention. They all have a core truth to them.

To walk what you talk is rare. If you ask most people what they think about divorce or adultery, the majority would say they're against it. The majority would also say they want to have a good relationship. Yet because so many people divorce, have affairs, or dislike their mate, the question becomes how can one have a good relationship?

I know that it is difficult, but possible, to have a loving and lasting relationship. I can tell you what has worked in my relationship with my husband and what I feel makes it successful. Some of the ideas I have may resonate with you and help you to discover that a great relationship is possible for you. You may find you can achieve what you desire. My grandmother's simple truths may help you accomplish that desire. They certainly helped me.

I'm writing this book as a woman who has learned through experience the difficulties and romance of walking the path of love and relationship and not as an expert in psychology. If I wanted to learn how to scuba dive I wouldn't take a class from someone who couldn't swim. Even if he'd read many books about the subject and had studied it for years, he wouldn't be my choice for an instructor. Nor would I jump in the water if I had no idea what I was doing. I would choose to learn from an experienced diver, someone who loves diving and does it all the time. The best teachers live what they do and practice what they preach. I can see proof of what they are doing by how they are living their lives and the success they are having. That's the best test that can be offered. My grandmother's Maxim #11 says it best, "The proof is in the pudding." This book is my pudding and its recipe is my life.

I used to think a good relationship was possible for everyone. When our eldest daughter was in nursery school, most of the parents of her fifteen classmates seemed happily married. By the time she was in second grade, not one of those couples was still married. People congratulated my husband and me like we had won a contest. "I can't believe you two are still together," was the usual response from someone we hadn't recently seen. I finally realized that our relationship is unusual. I could see obvious reasons why our marriage was so strong. What happened in those other relationships that had started so well, but ended so sadly? Why was it impossible for so many couples–made up of kind, gifted, loving people–to make sense of their lives together?

Why did so many end in divorce?

The ideas of divorce and separation have become the normal resolution to the many problems regarding difficulties in relationship. Applying this option of divorce or separation is all too easy. It exacts a type of self-fulfilling prophecy that assumes the fatal impossibility of making your relationship work.

I grew up in the fifties and sixties with divorced parents. I was the only person who came from a "broken home." The usual comment when I was in trouble was, "Well you know, her parents are divorced." Divorce was not the way to solve an unhappy marriage. People stayed married. Of course, many people also stayed miserable. The choice between divorce and being miserable is not much of a choice. Even the choice of having an "okay" relationship is not much of a choice. But there is another choice: choosing a great relationship.

I realize that's easy to say. The question is how do you do this? It takes a willingness and a daring to plant the seed of an alternative possibility and to tend this seed so it can grow. This is how my grandmother helped me with her wise sayings. Her wisdom planted seeds of possibility and practicality in me that allowed me to think for myself and to choose a great relationship. This was the gift that comes from recognizing that much of life is choice. It is both the assumption of what we think we are and what we believe we can become.

By tending the seed of relationship, you become a better you. My husband has told me many times that he would not be the person he is today without having experienced our relationship. I wasn't exactly sure what he meant at first. He is a pretty amazing guy and wouldn't he have turned out the same way on his own? He's positive he wouldn't have come close. I understand what he means. Our relationship has made us better individuals. We are better together than we ever were apart. Even though we have had our own difficulties, we try to influence one another in positive ways, helping each other grow to be the best we can be.

Our world could be a better place or at least vastly improved, if each of us tried to make the most of our personal relationships. When we become better people, we affect everyone around us in a more favorable manner. By striving to live in harmony, we would make the most of our lives while helping others do the same. I was given a great and lasting gift in the simple and practical wisdom expressed by my grandmother. In the spirit of sharing thoughts and ideas that can heal and inspire, I offer this book to you and hope that it affects your life in a positive way.

Chapter One

THE PURPOSE OF LIFE IS TO LOVE

Alice Through the Looking Glass

Some years ago, I was filming the movie *Point Break*. I'd been working on the skydiving sequences of the movie for a few weeks. For a particular shot the camera and operator were in a helicopter filming the skydivers in mid-air performing a stunt. I was in a twin otter airplane with the jumpers. We had an experienced crew of camera people, pilots and divers and yet, on a routine pass, the helicopter clipped the tail end of the plane. At the moment of impact, the plane jolted and someone yelled, "We're hit! We're going down!"

This could not be happening. Had I somehow been transported to a John Wayne World War II movie? Then the reality of the situation hit me. This plane was going to crash and I was going to die. I tried to brace myself and prepare for the worst, still unable to comprehend how this could be happening to me. I couldn't die now; I had barely begun to live.

The next thing I heard was, "Get out! Get out! Come on! Jump!"

Here was an alternative I hadn't considered. I was wearing a parachute as a safety requirement, but I had never jumped. I hadn't even thought about jumping, but it seemed like a great idea under the circumstances and out I went. I felt like Alice jumping through the looking glass. I went from the madness of the adrenaline frenzy inside the plane, through a roaring wind tunnel of oblivion as I jumped, to a huge shock of force as my parachute suddenly jerked open. And then silence. As I drifted alone in the still atmosphere ten thousand feet above the earth, I experienced an incredible godliness of complete serenity and peace. Suddenly, a large dark blob plunged past me. What was that? A person? No, I think I was the last person out of the plane. A part of the plane? I could no longer see the helicopter or the airplane. What had happened to them? And then nothing. The infinite silence embraced me once again. Maybe I had died. I felt a slight breeze on my face. I was still here although I wasn't exactly sure what was going to happen next.

I hung there in space for what seemed like an eternity. I didn't seem to be getting any closer to the ground. I peered down below me as carefully as I could. I didn't want to disturb what I thought might be a precarious balance. I saw little ant figures far below me with colorful chutes attached to them. They gracefully floated to the ground and the little ants rushed out from underneath them. What was this? One of the chutes, a round one, landed and no little ant ran out. The chute just laid there deflated with no life left in it.

I hadn't thought about landing. How did one accomplish this feat? Amazingly enough, I was still calm, an observer of this surreal scenario. Finally the figures below seemed to be getting larger. I was descending, after all, from my dangling dilemma. One large ant was running back and forth below me shouting incomprehensible words. The apparent urgency of the garbled sounds confused me. Finally the incomprehensible words became clear. "Steer towards the airport! Steer towards the airport!"

The airport? Where was the airport? Steer? I found out later that my large ant was trying to get me to head into the wind for a safer landing position.

I had one of the old circular parachutes that, to my knowledge, didn't have the toggles which control direction that the newer squares have. I found out later that it also didn't come with a reserve chute and was a handmade job one of the guys had put together in his garage and had never been used. I'm glad I didn't know this before jumping. Somehow my instincts took over. I searched the horizon for the airport buildings, found them, and managed to shift my weight enough to head towards them. I did this with some trepidation, as I had no idea what I was doing or what I should be doing and feared that if I moved at all, I might move something that shouldn't be moved.

And then I was down. My brain immediately switched gears to deal with the emergency at hand. Was everyone accounted for? What had happened to the guys in the helicopter? Everyone from the airplane was okay, except for a few minor injuries. I later found out the helicopter had sustained major damage, but the pilot had somehow managed to land, an amazing miracle for the cameraman and pilot inside. They had been sure they were going to plummet to the earth at any second and it had taken many seconds for them to descend. And yet, as soon as they landed, they both jumped into another helicopter to race out to find any survivors from the plane. They were sure we would all be scattered in many pieces on the ground. They were euphoric to find out everyone had made it. No one had disappeared through the looking glass.

Transformation

What had happened didn't register with me until a few days later after I had finished the job and was making the long drive back to Los Angeles. It was the first time I didn't have to think about a million other things. I had been extremely calm during and after the whole ordeal. I had called the studio to let them know what had happened and described the incident to them. The executive asked me who had to jump out of the plane. I listed all the names and added my own at the end. The executive was amazed. "You just jumped out of a crashing airplane and you're telling me all the details like you're reading a laundry list. How can you be so calm?"

I had also called my husband, Leigh, because I knew he would be worried if he heard the media reports.

"I just want to let you know I was in a mid-air collision and had to parachute out of the airplane. Everyone is okay and I'm fine so don't worry if you hear anything about it on the news. I have to get back to work. I love you and I'll see you soon."

There was a pause and then his response. "How did you like skydiving?"

He later told me that he had not really comprehended everything I had said until after he had hung up the phone. He was accustomed to me doing unusual things, but this one was definitely the topper so far. Little did he know that I would soon go to Kauai to film Steven Spielberg's *Jurassic Park* and be in the middle of a hurricane that devastated the island. Was the universe trying to tell me something? Just in case I didn't get the message, it was going to tell me again.

I did get the message. It started to come in loud and clear as I was driving home after the mid-air collision. I remembered what I had thought and felt when I had been confronted with death. Most people report the same feeling. They can't believe that death is imminent and happening to them. We all know we will die and yet we don't consider that it could occur until we are old and decrepit. It's reported that the most commonly said words of people on a crashing airplane are, "Oh shit," words that seem a sad resignation to the end of a life not yet fully lived. People think they'll live until ninety and have plenty of time to be and to do. What happened?

I remembered the large dark blob that had plummeted past me and seeing the parachute, a round one like the one that had suspended me in the air, deflate on the ground, but not seeing anyone emerge from it. When I asked the others about these incidents, no one else had seen either occur. I dismissed the events at the time, but now wondered what those visions could have possibly been. Had I perhaps seen my own death on another plane? (No pun intended.) Did I get a glimpse of what might have been? The fragility of life hit me. At first I was angry. What is the point when any one of us could be taken at any second? Why even bother? Life seemed so meaningless.

It finally dawned on me that this wasn't the message I was intended to receive. The message was that even if life could be taken from you at any moment, that doesn't mean you should give up and question the reason why you should live at all. It means that you should live life to its fullest, appreciate every moment that you are here, and not merely exist. Know what is important. I knew then that I would no longer have time for what is not important.

So what is important? Love is important. Grandma would often say, "The purpose of life is a life of purpose," Grandma's Maxim #79. That purpose is love. I believe it's why we are here, why we are human. You must learn and know love. You must give love and receive it back again; it's the essential ebb and flow of life.

Chapter Two

DO WE HAVE TO LEARN ABOUT LOVE
FROM OUR PARENTS?

Animals learn from their parents. They learn survival—how to swim, fly, hunt, gather their food, and defend themselves from predators.

We also learn from our parents. They can influence us in many ways. As young children we usually try to copy much of what we see mommy and daddy doing. They are our idols and we want to be like them. "Imitation is the sincerest form of flattery," Grandma's Maxim #80. How many little girls have dressed up in mommy's clothes and mimicked her behavior when playing house with their friends and dolls? We can learn a lot by watching our children imitate us. We smile at much of their mimicry and probably have our eyes opened to some rather unpleasant things we have said or done as well. Do we really sound like that? I've had a few surprises and have altered my behavioral patterns after seeing them played out by my children.

Unfortunately, many parents don't realize how much their behavior affects their children. Parents continue to argue in front of their children, treat their mates like idiots or show no affection for them whatsoever. Many feel that this learned behavior is the main reason for the terrible state of "broken homes" that we are experiencing in our society. We've learned about relationships from our parents and we continue to perpetuate their behaviors once we have our own relationships.

If I agreed with this idea, neither my husband nor I would have any chance at a successful marriage. My parents were married young and for all the wrong reasons. I think my mother wanted to prove she could win the prize of the handsome young man for a husband. My father was pressured by his father to get married to stay out of the war. My parents' marriage lasted eleven years, but it was filled with the game playing, lying, cheating and general mayhem that so often occurs when the inner child prevails and the inner adult is asleep.

I loved my father's response when I mentioned an old boyfriend of my mother's.

"That's the guy who broke up my marriage."

I was confused by his statement and mentioned to him that I thought both Mom and he had had their share of infidelities. He responded, "I might have had a lot of girlfriends, but none of them ever wrecked my marriage."

My father remarried and divorced two more times and continued to have many women in his life. Definitely not a good example for a relationship role model. My father had many good qualities, but fidelity wasn't one of them.

Mom didn't fare well in this department either. She was only married one other time after she left Dad, but she and her new husband not only had separate bedrooms, they had separate houses and dated occasionally. Although she never said it, I know she had never been in love because she often told me, "The only true love in a woman's life is the love she feels for her children. No one can love a man like that because your children are an actual part of you." I'm not sure where partner-in-life was relegated for her, but I realized I was lucky to be her daughter and not her husband.

Even though my parents were not exemplary role models for me, they affected my relationship with my husband in a positive way. I had definite proof of what did not work in a relationship and knew exactly what not to do, which in many cases can be a step in the right direction and saved me much heartache.

I was always involved in a relationship, but I never thought I would get married because I never thought I'd love someone enough to want to spend my life with him. This was a definite criterion for me and I wouldn't consider marriage without it. I remembered Grandma's Maxim #47, "When there is marriage without love, there will be love without marriage."

I believed you should only marry if you were sure it would be for life. It was something to be considered seriously and never entered into frivolously. I developed a strict viewpoint about marriage that ultimately served me well because I was completely in love and committed to my husband when I decided to marry him.

Love and Commitment

My husband, Leigh, and I were married by a minister who happened to be my brother-in-law. He came from Wisconsin to marry us in California. We met with him some days prior to our marriage for prenuptial counseling. Leigh and I did most of the talking in response to a few questions he proposed to us. We were obviously enthusiastic about our upcoming marriage which was reflected in our rather long dialogue. At the end of the session, my brother-in-law looked at us with amazement. I wasn't exactly sure what that glazed look in his eye meant. Was it because Leigh and I can be a bit verbose? He finally admitted he was amazed by how much hope and love we had. I was taken aback. Here was a man who had counseled hundreds of couples. I didn't think anything Leigh or I was saying was unusual. We were getting married. I assumed everyone would feel as we did, that everyone would have such love and commitment to each other. In fact, a great love for and commitment to each other are probably the most important aspects of a relationship and you would think, the most obvious. Yet, you'd be surprised by how many people marry without love for or any commitment to each other. Talk about a big handicap! You should definitely examine your love and commitment before you walk down the aisle, otherwise, why bother?

I was prepared to never get married and continue my life as I had with decent relationships, without completely committing to anyone. In fact, I didn't believe it was possible to love someone that much. To want to be with one person forever? Not in this life. But all my assumptions changed when I met Leigh. Thank goodness I somehow gleaned that marriage was something different. Who would want to invest that much of her life in someone she didn't really love?

Before getting married, examine your motives carefully and if you can't find love and commitment in there for a lifetime, don't do it. This is a basic rule not to be violated.

I don't know if my philosophy is a direct result of experiencing my parents' failure in marriage, but of course their relationship must have influenced my perspective. I had a wonderful childhood and my parents' failures with their own relationships did not affect me in a negative way. I enjoyed being with my father and even remember liking his girlfriends. Maybe I liked the variety. I also enjoyed being a big part of my mother's life and knowing how much she loved me. My parents did the best they could under the circumstances and I thank them for giving me life.

Taking Responsibility for a Good Relationship

Of course, it helps people in life if they come from a happy home as opposed to a dysfunctional one, but I don't feel this is a criterion for someone to have a good relationship. We must take responsibility for our own lives and quit blaming mom and dad for the mess they made of us. There should be a statute of limitations for parents. You can blame them for the first seven years of dysfunctional behavior once you leave home, but after that, they are free from culpability. What you do to mess up your life is your own responsibility. Accept this reality. People can do horrible things to you, but it's how you react to them that makes the difference. Your attitude is what is important. Refer to Grandma's Maxim #46, "The cup is half full, not half-empty" or #51, "See the doughnut, not the hole."

Parents seem to be the focus of blame whatever they do. There is a story about two people who had twin sons. The parents were perplexed because, even though their sons were identical, one of them was an eternal optimist and the other was a die-hard pessimist. The concerned parents asked a psychiatrist what they should do to help their sons get a more even perspective on life. The psychiatrist told them that for their sons' next birthday, they should give the pessimistic son everything he could possibly desire. The optimistic son should only get a pile of horse manure.

The parents followed the psychiatrist's advice and on the twins' next birthday delivered the appropriate gifts. They tiptoed to their pessimistic son's room and peeked in, expecting to see him thrilled with all his presents. Instead, they saw him throwing all his new toys on the floor and stomping around in a disgruntled manner.

"What do I want with all this stupid junk? I know my parents are up to something. They just want to buy my love, to purchase my affection with some cheap toys. Did they really think I would fall for such a stunt?"

The parents were mortified, but nevertheless, they continued on to their optimistic son's room. When they peered in his door, they saw this son skipping gleefully around the large pile of horse manure and laughing joyfully exclaiming, "Where there's horse manure, there must be a pony!"

It's time to accept the fact that maybe we are the way we are because that's how we have chosen to be, how we have reacted to our life. This is not to say that you can't change. Grandma often quoted, "What you are is God's gift to you, what you make of it is your gift to God," Maxim #54.

There have been many books written about the awakening of our inner child. I suggest we get that inner adult awake real fast. All the blame for your life is not out there. In fact, forget blame altogether. Examine what isn't working. Give yourself permission to start changing your behavior. Take responsibility for your relationship. More importantly, take responsibility for yourself. You're probably thinking that that's a lot easier said than done. Remember Grandma's Maxim #17, "The person who says it can't be done should not interrupt the person doing it." If it drives you crazy when your mate leaves wet towels on the bathroom floor, tell him. Don't keep it inside letting resentment fester. Maybe your mother always kept her feelings inside and never expressed them, only growing angrier every day. But you can react differently.

You know her way didn't work for her or for you, so learn from it. Start expressing yourself.

If your mate knows you hate that he leaves wet towels around, and he still does it after much discussion and nagging, pick the towels up yourself. Is it that big of a deal to argue about constantly? I'm all for standing up for what you believe, but choose important issues upon which to make your stand. After all, we have to be willing to throw in the towel now and then.

If you always leave the towels on the floor and it drives your mate crazy, try picking them up. Make yourself pick them up. Once again, not a big issue. Start small. Be willing to let something go that is not that important. A little effort in changing a pattern can produce changes in yourself and your mate as your efforts are noted. A little effort in accepting your mate's irritating habits can go a long way also. Grandma's advice would apply here. "Keep your eyes wide open before marriage and half shut after marriage," Maxim #57. Quit harping. Stop making both of you miserable.

Learning What Not To Do

I once read a book that said people choose their parents. I know that statement alone provokes skepticsm, but nevertheless, it made me think. Some assertions, even if they are against your particular beliefs, religious or otherwise, are interesting to explore as they can illuminate many aspects of your life. After reading this statement, I often contemplated why I would choose the particular people I had chosen for my parents. I must have needed them for a special purpose. I came up with various answers, but none were entirely satisfactory. One day the answer became very clear and simple: "To learn what not to do." Clear and concise, this made sense to me. We all know mistakes are made. Sometimes we do stupid or even despicable things. The point is to not continue this behavior, but to learn from it.

I tell my children that if they do something wrong, they should never try to hide it or lie about it. Besides, "A liar needs a good memory," Grandma's Maxim #60. They know I'll get upset about the lie, but not the mistake. The important thing is to realize what went wrong and what needs to be fixed to make things right. Then fix it. People mess up. It's what they do afterwards that counts.

My parents actually helped me. I could look at their lives, see what they did that didn't work and try to make sure I didn't make the same mistakes. They actually saved me the trouble of making those mistakes myself. Of course many people go right ahead and make the same mistakes anyway. They are somehow programmed to believe they can't avoid their parents' fate. The trick is to learn from the mistakes you witness. When you see how dysfunctional certain behavior is, avoid that behavior. It doesn't work and you know it. You've seen it first hand. Learn from the mistakes of others.

Your parents don't have to have the perfect marriage or be the perfect parents for you to have a successful relationship. They don't have to be your role models. There are many people who have horrible relationships who actually had parents with good marriages. Unless you've been living on a desert island alone or locked in a closet, you know at least the basic behavior that works in a relationship.

We've all seen bad relationships; a few of us have seen good ones. We've seen how both are portrayed in movies, TV, books, etc. We also know a lot about both innately. We know what it's like to be kind to someone; we also know what it's like to be nasty. Hitting someone is bad. Cheating on them is also bad. Helping someone is good. We see how others react to our behavior; it can be as simple as making them smile or cry. So let's stop blaming mom and dad's horrible relationship for our horrible relationship. "I never learned how to love," doesn't cut it. Even if I accepted this excuse, it can be changed right now. You can change. Learn how to love now.

~ It all depends on you. You must take responsibility for your relationship. You can start your relationship so it has a chance of surviving, i.e. with love and commitment.

~ You can fix it if it has a few holes or even if the bottom seems to have fallen out of it.

~ You can get that inner adult busy learning from past mistakes and changing your behavior. After you begin doing the hard work, the inner child can come out and play and really have fun. She won't have to pout all day or have a temper tantrum. She can smell a rose, climb a tree, marvel at a sunset, tickle someone mercilessly.

~ Stop blaming others for all the reasons your relationship isn't working. Who cares whose fault it is? It doesn't help you at all. You stay exactly where you are. Even if you say it's your mate's fault, you're still miserable because nothing has changed. You must find the strength to move on if you want things to change.

~ You can change.

~ Practice what you learn and know about having a good relationship. That would be Grandma's Maxim #59, "Practice makes perfect."

Chapter Three

HOW DO I FIND SOMEONE TO LOVE?

Most people ask how can I find someone to love me? This is part of the problem. People want someone to love them, but they don't necessarily think about loving someone else. We are back to that inner child again: I want what I want when I want it. It seems difficult to think of others, to care about their needs, to give when taking is much easier. Our own needs and desires come first and finding someone to love us seems to be foremost in our minds.

What characteristics in a mate matter most to us if we are really honest? Wealthy probably pops into mind quickly, and of course attractive. This criteria excludes quite a few people and makes our task of finding someone to love even more daunting. We may also say kind, loyal, a good sense of humor, smart, but let's examine how those first two qualifications put us in a debit situation before we even try to have a relationship.

Show Me the Money

An interesting phenomenon occurring more frequently with many of my female peers is that they now say they want to find someone who can take care of them. These are women who were concerned with women's rights and active in the women's movement. The general prerequisite for this "someone" is that he must be rich or at least have definite prospects of becoming wealthy. These women were independent and knew they had much to offer the world. For them to now want to be taken care of is a definite change of values. I'm sure we all want, need, and should be taken care of at times, but to have this as a main focus in a relationship is not a positive sign. The idea of two is inherent in relationship. If one of those two only wants to be on the receiving end, it does not bode well for a sharing relationship.

I grew up with the idea that a woman should marry a rich man and I remember my mother being especially fond of a new boyfriend I had met while traveling in Europe. She didn't know much about him except that he was a doctor and therefore must be wonderful. I was encouraged to accept an invitation to visit him in California once I returned home from Europe. Even my Grandmother, who was prim and proper, seemed to agree. An unchaperoned visit to a gentleman's home! Lordy, lordy Gram, what would people think?

A similar situation occurred when I attended university in Madrid, Spain. I lived with a conservative family. They set the rules from the beginning of my stay that I must always tell them where I was going, when I would return, with whom I was going out, etc. On a flight from Mallorca to Madrid, I met an older, aristocratic gentleman. My Spanish family was impressed when I told them the name of my new companion. When this gentleman invited me to join him on a trip to the Canary Islands some months later, they encouraged me to go. I expected my sensible, conservative family to deem such a trip inappropriate, but they told me that a young lady did not often have an opportunity for such advantages in life.

The advice given in each of these situations made me feel dishonorable, as if I was being encouraged to sell myself to the highest bidder. The idea repulsed me. I had always supported myself and never relied on anyone. If money was going to be important to me, I realized early on that I had better make it myself and not think someone else was going to do it for me. This is a basic tenet I have always had and one I was proud that my fellow women seemed to follow.

One day I heard a conversation between my daughter, Brighton, and her young friend. They were discussing their future plans, at age eight. Brighton's friend remarked that she was going to marry a rich man. Brighton replied that she was going to make her own money, then she could marry anyone she wanted. Sounds like a better solution to me. If money is important to you, take Brighton's advice—do your best to make it yourself.

I had recently read the story of Hercules to Brighton and maybe it had influenced her decision. It's a good story for all of us to note.

When Hercules was eighteen, he started thinking about his future life. As he pondered, he saw, or thought he saw, two women approaching him. One ran ahead to get the first word with him. She was tall and handsome and finely dressed. She told him that she knew he was doubtful about what he should do and what path of life he should take. She said that if he would follow her, he would have the easiest and most pleasant life in the world, a life with no hard work and nothing to worry about. Others would have to work, but he would be as happy as the day is long. When Hercules asked her name, she replied that her real name was Pleasure, but her enemies called her Vice.

By this time, the second woman had arrived. She was also tall and handsome, but in a different way. She was stately and dignified and looked very noble. Her dress was all white, truth was in her eyes, and modesty in her manners. She told Hercules that she would not deceive him with promises of pleasant things, but would tell him the truth. He would never get anything worthwhile for himself unless he worked for it. He must plow and sow and reap in order to enjoy the fruits of the earth. If he wanted a strong body, he must make his body the servant of his mind and fear not labor and sweat. In the same way, if he wanted the love of friends, he must be kind to his friends; if he wanted honor from his city or country, he must work for their benefit. If he followed her, he would be truly happy. Her name was Virtue.

Pleasure said Hercules would never have any fun if he followed Virtue, but Virtue reminded him that Pleasure's promise of ease only led to excess and weariness: he who tried to be happy on such a path never succeeded, but he who did noble deeds gained happiness without trying.

I realize the old work ethic is not always attractive to us, but nonetheless, it seems to hold true.

So, what has gone wrong? What happened to those ideals of working hard, taking care of yourself, and making your own decisions in life for all the right reasons? Did the women's movement decide to hang a right on Easy Street and give up what women have strived so hard to achieve? Do women only want equal rights with men on their own terms and not for the long term? Many women have become weary. They have worked all this time and now just want someone else to do it for a while. I can understand this and there is nothing wrong with it. However, in a relationship, both partners need to take care of themselves and each other. In a relationship, both partners need to give and to work together, hopefully for similar goals.

I'm not excusing men from the "I want someone to take care of me" syndrome either. Many of my male friends seem to get that look of love a little easier, or maybe become blind to a few trouble spots when the latest object of their attention is a successful business woman or one who comes from money. It just seems that women tend to fall into this trap more easily because it has been more acceptable for women to be in the receiving position. The problem is that a lot of prospective partners are overlooked when we have this goal in mind.

I know at least five men who had relationships cool very quickly when the women they were dating realized they were not wealthy and their prospects for earning were not auspicious. As much as these men would like a relationship, they cannot give up their passion as an artist or a writer to focus on earning money. Money isn't that important to them and they are dedicated to and love what they do. These are men who appear to be great partners in life, men who should be admired. They have ideals and talent and yet many women will not commit to them because they want the men to show them the money. For many people the idea of a partner having no money isn't acceptable. The idea of working together to create what they want isn't foremost in their minds. They no longer have time to wait around. They want an easy life now.

If you're tired of working hard, take a vacation, even a long vacation, but don't throw in the towel and say, "Sold to the highest bidder." Don't make money your big priority in finding a mate. There are too many good people who don't have much green stuff, but have a lot of gray matter and great big hearts. I find the latter much more bankable in the long run.

You don't need to run away from someone who has money, but have a relationship with him because of who he is and not because of what he has. Don't let the money lead you, let your soul lead you. I'm aware of many a mother's advice, "You can fall in love with a rich man just as easily as a poor one." We all know that is not necessarily so. If you are truly in love I think you can make it together. We also know "Money can't buy happiness," Grandma's Maxim #30. You can argue that poverty can't buy happiness either and you would be right. The point is, money, or the lack of it, doesn't make a good relationship. Love makes a good relationship. Being with each other is what is important. If money is important to you, make it yourself.

Creative Sharing of Financial Responsibilities

My husband, Leigh, is an actor, artist and author. None of these is the most secure of professions. We met while working on a show called *Executive Suite* and Leigh was making a good living at the time. I was not earning much as an assistant director trainee, but I had good prospects and all the money I felt I needed because I never had any time to spend it anyway. *Executive Suite* was canceled after twenty-two shows, my first dose in a long line of Grandma's Maxim #63, "Easy come, easy go."

When Leigh and I moved into our new apartment together, our worldly possessions consisted of a piano and a mattress. I think they were both his. I had given all my things to a former boyfriend, probably out of guilt after leaving him. I never thought about how much Leigh was going to make nor how much money he had. I'm sure he could have cared less about my bank account. We never thought of keeping our own money and dividing expenses. I know many couples do this, but it never occurred to us. We were living together and would do so in every sense of the word. Later, when we had accumulated a bit more than the piano and mattress, we were advised by a business manager to keep our money separate. We could not conceive of the idea. Who would do that? Our business manager had been married several times and was trying to give us sound advice. We didn't take it. If you are in this for life, share the money, even if you are the one who has most of it.

Leigh and I both worked, not always at the same time. It turned out to be a great system and one we still use to this day. Neither of us have given up our careers, we alternate them. We both feel that we contribute financially to our life together. Once we had children, this worked out well because one of us was always with them. They were never left solely to the care of a nanny. We could have had more money and advanced further in our careers if we had both worked all the time, but we would have lost so much by not spending the time with our children and each other. I could have made the decision to always stay home, but I have seen the benefits of sharing the responsibilities of earning a living.

There wasn't always a choice in who had to work. Sometimes it was whoever had the opportunity to get a job. Both of us have given up jobs we may have desired or accepted less desirable ones. When I returned to work after being with our eldest daughter, Caytlyn, for her first year and a half, it was difficult for me. However, it ended up being positive for all of us. Caytlyn and Leigh developed a wonderful relationship as Leigh became the best Mr. Mom around and I was taking care of them both by earning a living.

Our careers are perhaps more adapted to this arrangement, but it is possible for anyone to do what we do. Much can be learned in any arena by switching positions with someone else, be it at work, home or play. You develop a new understanding of what the other person must endure. You have new respect for what he does. "You cannot judge a man unless you have walked a mile in his shoes," Grandma's Maxim #87.

A favorite childhood story I read many times was a Bohemian tale about a husband and wife who decided to switch jobs. The husband thought his wife did nothing in the house while he slaved away in the fields all day. However, he was completely overwhelmed with all she did when he tried to take her place. The baby cried continuously, the house was left in shambles when all sorts of mishaps occurred and the cow ended up on the roof. I think that cow on the roof was my favorite part. Of course the story didn't relate what adjustments the woman had to make to get through the day (it must have been written by an early Bohemian women's libber), but I'm sure she had new respect for her husband's work as well.

Be creative with your ideas about sharing the financial responsibilities. You can find a solution. Remember Grandma's Maxim #66, "An obstacle is something you see when you take your eyes off the goal." It doesn't have to be fifty/fifty either as far as the monetary reward is concerned. Don't become obsessed with, "I made more money than you." If you're both trying to do what needs to be done, you're on the right track. Remember, you're working for the benefit of the whole, not for the benefit of yourself. Stop being consumed with self-adulation. There is a relationship to consider and it doesn't bode well if you're pointing out how much more you're contributing to the coffers than your mate. Remember you're a team.

If you feel your profession would never allow such an arrangement, then think about alternatives more seriously. As an assistant director I introduced the idea of job sharing in the Directors Guild of America. Most people thought job sharing was odd because no one had done it before, but it has worked well for me. You don't have to be constantly away from your family; you have a few days off to be with them. This arrangement benefits employers because they're working with someone who isn't completely stressed over responsibilities at home and work or someone who is exhausted from trying to handle both. The production company gets two people and their creative ideas for the price of one. Of course, you earn less money than you would working all the time. Once again, it all depends on your priorities and your needs. "Necessity is the mother of invention," Grandma's Maxim #85. It's surprising how inventive you can become when you put your mind to it and realize what's important.

Leigh and I don't want one another to fail at anything. If you and your mate share responsibilities, you'll both be familiar with running the home and business aspects of your lives so you can easily switch positions. I know quite a few couples that use this arrangement more and more and I see great things come from it. My favorite is the relationship fathers have with their children when they are the primary caregivers. Remember Grandma's Maxim #81, "Every calling is great when greatly pursued." This applies to the calling of breadwinner or breadmaker. By the way, most of the couples I know who share responsibilities agree being at home is the most demanding job, but the one they care about the most.

Looking Deeper

Most of us have a difficult time with Grandma's Maxim #27, "It's what's inside that counts." How many of us have run in the opposite direction when our friends try to set us up with someone who has a great personality? We know they will be dogs. Most of us could never fathom falling in love with an unattractive person because we would never give him the time of day to even find out if he could speak. By doing this, we are once again limiting the prospects of meeting people that could greatly add to our lives.

My husband and I attended a weekend seminar early in our relationship. After the introductory meeting, I remember remarking to Leigh that I thought the people at the seminar seemed strange. I determined this strictly by looking at everyone in the audience. In this first meeting I had not heard anyone speak, nor had I interacted with anyone. I decided I wouldn't be interested in this group apparently because they didn't look the way I thought they should. As the weekend progressed I heard many of these people speak, shared thoughts and ideas with them and gradually became acquainted with them. I don't remember what this particular conference was about, but I remember clearly that by the end of the weekend, the same people I had earlier dismissed had become fascinating to me. They were intelligent, insightful, interesting and attractive. Their very forms seemed to change for me.

I hadn't consciously decided to accept the people for who they were, it had just happened. I had spent some time with them and listened to them and they were magically transformed from frogs into princes. I learned a most valuable lesson from this seminar and it had nothing to do with the topic for the weekend. Perhaps I finally understood

Grandma's Maxim #64, "Character is what you are in the dark." I know I'm not alone in this experience. There are men and women out there who have much to offer, but they are overlooked because of their outward appearance. As Grandma would have said, "You must look into people as well as at them," Maxim #33.

One of my girlfriends was married quite young to someone she thought was gorgeous. She had often told me she couldn't have a relationship with someone who wasn't good-looking. After she and her husband were divorced for a few years, she confessed to me that she now often looked at couples walking hand-in-hand and envied their relationship. She wanted a relationship with a good person and she didn't care how he looked. This was a major change for her that had come about from a difficult lesson, but she learned from her misfortune and made the necessary changes in her attitude and life. She has been with a great guy now for about twelve years. He isn't good-looking, but she's the happiest I've ever seen her.

Why do we set these standards? Some of us are not exactly gorgeous ourselves and yet we convince ourselves that our dream mate must be. Isn't it another form of vanity and ego? We must only be with attractive people because they reflect on us. Hopefully we don't have to be as shallow as the people we think we are impressing. Dig deeper; know there is more.

Be Careful What You Wish For, You Might Just Get It

Once you get over the hurdle of excluding more than half the population because they are not rich or handsome, start thinking seriously about what you really do value in a mate. Go back to that list of noble qualities and choose which are important to you. Start picturing the kind of person with whom you would want to spend the rest of your life. Do some soul searching. You may learn about yourself and what you value in life in the process. Be specific.

Recognize thought is energy and when you have a clear picture of what you want in life, that thought or energy can be sent out into the universe to attract and manifest what you desire. Following this premise, I have had some amazing things occur. God does answer prayers. Visualizing does work. However you want to put it, our lives are full of amazing coincidences.

These coincidences happen in many ways. Some of us are lucky and good things just seem to come our way. Others spend time meditating or praying and feel that helps them a great deal. Others feel they are doomed and nothing will help them. For those in the last category I would recommend taking a few moments each day to relax your body, breathe deeply, clear your mind of all the clutter that has accumulated and engage in a form of meditation or mindfulness.

Some people say prayer is speaking to God and meditation is listening to God. I say do whatever works for you. There are different types of meditation practices. Sometimes I just still my mind and listen to whatever may be revealed to me. You can ask a question such as, "What do I need to know right now?" It may take some time to get a response, but don't give up. I don't know if it's your inner voice that speaks or the universe or some other form of divine consciousness, but I seem to eventually get guidance from this method. You may sit quietly and not ask about anything at all. Do whatever works best for you. I guarantee that at the very least you will end up feeling more relaxed and focused. Your thoughts come together and you don't feel scattered in the wind. You feel healthier. It can't hurt you and I've seen only positive results.

At other times I practice a form of visualization. I see what I'd like to happen as clearly as possible. I imagine every detail of it and perceive it as already existing. I'm there. As I've said before, it's necessary to be specific. There was a person who wanted a new car. In her meditations she concentrated on getting a new car. Unfortunately, a tree fell on her old car so she had to get a new car. That's not exactly the scenario she had in mind.

A young lady I know had a crush on the boy next door ever since she could remember. Alas, her love was unrequited and he barely knew she existed. She started visualizing being with him. She was a romantic young lady and what she pictured was herself in a flowing gown and her young man in a tuxedo dancing at a ball. He was holding her in his arms in a "Fred and Ginger" pose to make the picture in her mind complete. Their lives continued separately, with him giving her an occasional nod of recognition, always cordial, but not much more. She became disillusioned with her visualization and gave up on the idea altogether. In their senior year of high school she and her heartthrob were both elected to prom court as their class representatives. She ended up having a fantastic evening with him, dancing the night away in a very romantic setting, gown and all (I have the picture to prove it). She didn't have a romantic relationship with this young man and still thinks visualizing is silly. I say she experienced exactly what she had pictured, although it does reveal that the universe has a sense of humor.

This is an important point. Listen to Grandma's Maxim #23,

"Be careful what you wish for, you might just get it" or perhaps #39, "There are two tragedies in life. One is not to get your heart's desire. The other is to get it." That's why you must examine what you think is your dream. Go for the gold. Brass tarnishes easily. How many people do you know who have felt their lives would be perfect if only they could be with John or Jane? They end up with Jane, who has a drinking problem and loves to fight, or John, who is jealous and selfish and an emotional basket case. Couldn't they see what was occurring? They say they were blinded by love or they thought the person would change once they were together. It's easy to be naive or ignore what we prefer not to see, but with the help of our inner voice, if we work to cultivate it, we can be honest with ourselves and discerning of others.

Many of us have ignored this voice for so long that it doesn't seem to exist anymore. It's possible to awaken this voice, just try listening to it. Take some time to let it speak to you and guide you. I don't always listen to my voice when I should, but it's there. Sometimes it is slightly vexed by my behavior, "What are you doing, are you crazy?" Other times it cautions me, "Something isn't right here. Take your time and think this one out." Call it intuition, conscience, guardian angel, whatever name you prefer, but listen to it. It can serve you well.

I know many people who practice a type of visualization in all sorts of situations. It can be as minor as getting a parking place on a crowded street. They see an empty space in their minds and voila!, another car is pulling out just in time for them to take the vacated area. My friends report great success with this one. In fact these insignificant desires of ours seem to occur quite readily if we take the time to notice. Maybe it's because we don't attach that much importance to them. The difficult ones, like being in the ideal relationship, seem to take longer. Sometimes a lot longer.

Fix Yourself First

My friend, Elaine, wasn't the happiest person after her divorce. I would tell her to be positive and thankful and to see herself in a loving relationship. She followed my advice for a long time and yet she had few relationships, none she really cared for. This went on for years and when she was discouraged, she often told me how ridiculous it was. She finally became involved in her career, her children, and realized life was full for her as a single person. She was far from content, but had made great strides in getting her life together. In her own way, she had stopped thinking a relationship was going to solve all her problems and fix her life. She had concentrated on fixing her life herself and becoming a whole person.

This is an important point. Too often we want someone to love us so we can be happy. We think a relationship will fix us and our lives. Everything will be okay once someone loves us. We forget that we cannot look outside to solve our problems. We must be whole people with fulfilling lives in order to have good relationships. "Do not put the cart before the horse," Grandma's Maxim #88. A relationship isn't the magic cure-all that will fix you. You must fix you.

Perfect Timing

One day Elaine received a call from Michael, a man she had known years before. Elaine and Michael were married a year ago. They both agree that if they had dated within the first few years after Elaine's divorce, they probably wouldn't have ended up together. They each had children from a previous marriage and needed to be full-time parents. Michael wasn't ready to commit to a relationship and had issues he needed to face by himself. Elaine had her own issues. It seems that these two came together at the most propitious time for both of them.

A dear friend of mine, Jan, is an art therapist. She often uses visualization in her practice and life. She draws her dreams and cuts out pictures of her ideal mate and environment. She was divorced and wanted to meet "Mr. Right." She asked me if I'd ever met anyone at work I thought she might find interesting. One day when I was working on a short project a new camera operator caught my eye. I knew this was the guy for my friend, Jan. I started asking the camera operator questions and I'm sure he thought I was hitting on him. I guess the "Are you married or seeing anyone special?" question made him wonder about my intentions. I immediately called Jan and said I had found the guy for her.

As luck would have it, I never succeeded in having them meet. The camera operator only worked on the show a couple of days and Jan had to leave town for a few weeks. Jan joked with me that it probably wouldn't have worked out anyway because I had told her she wouldn't meet Mr. Right until she was forty-one and she was only thirty-eight. I didn't remember telling her that, but you'll be surprised by the latent insights you develop when you meditate and open up the access to your inner voice. You plug into the universe and it flows through you. You start to see and feel many new sensations. Try to focus your energies in that direction. Just don't try too hard. You'll be surprised by what can happen.

Many times what you want seems to come to you after you have let it go and are not as attached to an outcome. My eldest daughter, Caytlyn, gets frustrated because few of her significant desires occur. Her insignificant wishes always come to fruition. I tell her not to fixate on a certain desire and constantly meditate on it or pray about it. Just put it out there and release it. Remember that you can't grasp water; you can only contain it gently in the palm of your hand. My daughter's results confirm this idea. She doesn't fixate on those unimportant desires. Now we only need to learn how to be less attached to important wishes. It's difficult, but not impossible.

Back to my friend, Jan. A week before she turned forty-two she met Mr. Right in a health food restaurant where she frequently goes for lunch. They fell in love faster than any couple I have known and decided to get married. I had not met him yet, so she invited me to have dinner with them one evening before the wedding. I was surprised when I walked in and was greeted by the camera operator from the show I had worked on years before. Once again, timing is everything.

Meeting Mr./Ms. Right

Now that you have your ideas clear about the type of person you would like and your own life is in order, where do you go to meet the person with whom you want to spend the rest of your life? Chances are he's not going to ring your doorbell while you're sitting at home watching TV. I believe anything is possible, but I would not put much faith in that scenario unless you have something interesting occurring at your home.

Unfortunately, if you have not met your mate in college or through your job, it becomes more difficult for many of us to encounter an interesting person. After working all day, we are tired and have no desire to go out. If you don't have the type of job where you meet new people, force yourself to leave your home. Even if you are tired or have a lot to do, you can make some time to get out and broaden your horizons. What do you like to do? What are your main interests? What type of person do you want to meet? These questions should give you a clue as to where to spend your time away from home.

I suggest vounteering or taking a class in which you are interested whether it is investment banking or rock climbing. Not only will you meet people with whom you have something in common, they will be people who are interested in learning, which is always a good sign. Someone who likes to learn will grow and be stimulating.

Many people think the grocery store is a great place for meeting people. I've never been able to tell much about a person by how he squeezes a tomato, but maybe you'll have better luck. It's too broad an area for me. After all, everyone has to eat. It also doesn't give you much time to get to know someone, especially if you shop in mini-markets.

Taking a trip is always a great way to meet new people. Airports used to be good meeting places, although they are a little crowded these days and people are always in such a hurry. Traveling is sure to be successful for meeting new people. Even if you don't meet your perfect person, think of what a great time you will have.

My favorite place for meeting people is a bookstore. Leigh and I met many of the interesting people we know in a bookstore. You might think this idea is terribly stodgy, but you would be surprised at the people you meet. Try it before you reject it. Remember there are many different sections in the bookstore and you can browse in any of them.

Some of the people we meet in bookstores come to the discussion groups we have in our home twice a week. Joining such a group is another good place to meet people. It all depends on your interests. Many people take part in church groups, political organizations or animal rights activities. My husband started our groups. I admire salons where people gather and present their art, writing, or thoughts. Leigh loves to discuss new ideas and engage in enlightening conversations. Consequently our Tuesday and Thursday evening discussion groups were born. We always have new people joining us and find these evenings fulfilling. Fascinating people can show up at your door. They do at our home every week, so we don't have to leave home to form interesting new relationships. I told you anything is possible.

Many turn to the Internet to find a partner. This could be a good or bad experience. I know quite a few people who love it and have married the person they met online, while others insist that they have never met anyone they consider relationship material. Obviously there is no one size fits all here. There are many online dating services and I say, why not give one a try? Just be wise about it. The good news is that people who use Internet services are probably interested in having a relationship. In a way, if you do connect with someone through correspondence or conversation before you meet in person, it can give the whole process an old time courting vibe, which in this day of high technology is perhaps a bit ironic.

~ How do you find someone to love? Start thinking about giving love instead of taking it.

~ Don't eliminate over half the population with vacuous criteria for a mate.

~ If money is important to you, make it yourself.

~ If you're in this for life, share the money, even if you're the one who has most of it.

~ If looks are important to you, look deeper and see how looks can change.

~ Get your priorities in order by examining them and yourself.

~ Don't make the mistake of thinking a relationship will fix your life.

~ Fix your life and yourself first.

~ Meditate and listen to your inner voice.

~ Determine what is important to you.

~ Let the universe know what you want so it can help you help yourself.

~ Realize the universe has its own timing.

~ "Seek and ye shall find," Grandma's Maxim #86.

~ Go places where you can meet interesting people.

~ Don't stay at home unless you have something occurring that will draw people to you.

~ Listen to Grandma's Maxim #34, "The journey of a thousand miles begins with one step."

Chapter Four

GETTING THE WHEEL GOING
IN THE RIGHT DIRECTION

Do the Right Thing

The most important thing you can do once you meet someone is what I call getting the wheel going in the right direction. It's never too early and rarely too late. In Grandma's words, "A stitch in time saves nine," Maxim #82, or "Better late than never," Grandma's Maxim #83. When you first start dating someone it's easy to accomplish this task. When the romance ebbs (which doesn't have to occur), it becomes more difficult. It's a basic principle in getting along with someone and you would think, easy to do.

Wheels go forward and backward. When wheels move forward, people do kind things for each other. They are considerate. They help whenever they can. They compliment each other. They show each other true affection. It can be something as simple as, "I noticed you had grease on your favorite pants so I cleaned them for your appointment tomorrow." Or it could be something more difficult, such as, "I gave Jane my ticket to Paris because I know you need me to stay with your mother and her cats in Irvine for the week." Moving the wheel forward is going out of your way to do something considerate for someone because you love him. You care about making him happy. You don't try to get any perks out of your good deeds for yourself. This is strictly a nice guy thing.

There are times we know we could do something to put a smile on our mate's face, but we are too busy. We have to take care of ourselves. Somehow we fail to notice our partners needs. If you want a good relationship, it's time to be kind and do considerate things for your mate.

What occurs once you start to be kind and to do considerate things for your mate? Interestingly, he'll probably begin doing kind and considerate things for you. Grandma's Maxim #3 is applicable here, "To have a friend, be one" or in this case, "To have a great partner, be one." This will happen unless you are with someone who has a heart and head made of stone or someone who is the most egocentric person on the planet and a user of other people. If you are with such a person, break up before you get married. Typically, people react positively when someone is kind to them. It makes them feel good. They like to be with people who make them happy. They want to do something considerate in return.

We all tend to reciprocate positively to good deeds even if we do it from a sense of propriety. "The Andersons had us over for dinner last week, so we'll have them over on Thursday." "Mary has driven our child to dance class so many times. We will take the girls to camp this week." We aren't even in love with the Andersons or Mary. It's just the natural thing to do. It should be inherent for us to do this with the person we love. This is the person with whom we have chosen to spend the rest of our life. So why can this be difficult?

We can make the wheel spin in the wrong direction. On our first anniversary, we buy flowers and have a beautiful candlelit dinner. Somehow we progress rapidly to forgetting the date altogether. We start complaining, criticizing, and assigning blame. We not only neglect to help our mate clean the house, we make more of a mess, leaving our dirty dishes on the table or our clothes all over the bedroom. Your wife won't have a warm cuddly feeling for you after you announce to your dinner guests how messy the house is and it's amazing she finally decided to clean it up. The next thing you know, she is complaining that you don't earn enough money and are a failure. She is criticizing the way you dress and blaming you because you forgot to water the garden and all the plants are dead. Grandma would tell you, "What goes around, comes around," Maxim #61.

No-Fault Marriage Insurance

I would love to give my friend, Erin, no-fault marriage insurance. This would be an insurance where neither person in a relationship can be blamed for anything. Erin has been married for twenty-nine years. Her husband, Rick, has been away on business for twenty-five of the twenty-nine. My friend and her husband blame each other for everything. If Rick had filled up the car with gas, Erin wouldn't have run out while returning that horrible shirt he bought. If Erin had gone to the grocery store, Rick wouldn't have run out of coffee and ended up late for work because he had to stop and pick some up, not to mention the fender-bender he had in the parking lot that is going to raise their insurance rates sky high.

Don't Erin and Rick realize this is a two-party system? Did Erin forget how to read a gas gauge? Why couldn't Rick go to the grocery store? Besides, as Grandma would say, "Things happen," Maxim #14. Sometimes people forget to do things or make mistakes. It's no one's fault and it wasn't done on purpose. Who cares anyway? Does it make it go away if you blame someone else? No. Now you not only have a dented fender, but an unhappy mate. Things only get worse. The wheel keeps spinning faster and faster in the wrong direction.

Think how things could have been different for Erin and Rick if they realized that neither of them was at fault? They both could have regretted the accident and comforted each other; they both could have thought of a way to get cheaper insurance; they both could have been united against the difficulty that had befallen them.

Each of them could have realized that together, supporting each other, they could deal with almost anything. Bad things do happen and nine times out of ten they are not anyone's fault. For that tenth time, who really cares? Blame solves nothing. You can only find a solution to a problem by working together to find a remedy and not alienating the one person who could help you the most in the middle of a crisis.

Many years ago I read a story to my youngest daughter, Brighton, about a man and wife who lived in a cottage high on a windy hill. One evening the man had just settled himself in his rocking chair with his pipe in his mouth and the wife had just begun to prepare their supper, when a gust of wind pushed open their cottage door. The windows rattled and the dishes on the cupboard shelves danced. Neither the man nor his wife would get up and close the door. They each felt it was not his fault the door had blown open and insisted the other should do it. They ended up in a big fight and refused to speak to each other, saying that whoever spoke first would have to close the door. The man sat in his chair and shivered. The woman tried to keep her teeth from chattering as she went about making supper. Neither of them shut the door.

Presently the woman placed her husband's supper on the table, but she didn't ask her husband to come to eat, so he just sat there.

A thief came along. He poked his head in at the open door. The man and the woman made no move, each still in a big huff. The thief stepped cautiously into the cottage. All remained quiet. The thief then sat down at the table and ate the whole supper. Then he gathered all the spoons and knives and forks together and put them into his pouch.

"These two must be deaf and dumb and blind," he said to himself. "What else can I take?"

His eyes went around the room and soon spotted the woman's best china teapot.

"Now, there's something," he said aloud. "That should fetch a pretty penny."

As he reached for the teapot, the woman finally burst out at the top of her lungs,

"Thief! Isn't it enough that you have eaten the whole supper and stolen all our silver? Must you have my best teapot too?"

Her cries startled their dog and cat so much that they both jumped up, the cat hissing and spitting and the dog growling and barking. As for the thief, he was so astonished at all the sudden noise that he was frightened out of his wits. He dropped the teapot, clutched the silver tightly to him, and ran off, the dog and cat following him in pursuit.

"After them, man!" cried the woman. "Will you sit there and do nothing while we lose everything?"

The stubborn man, with all the food gone, the silver stolen, and the best teapot in a thousand pieces on the floor only shrugged his shoulders and said,

"Wife, you spoke first. Now go and close the door."

Brighton and I both agreed that this was indeed a silly story. Who would act this way? As silly as this story is however, behavior like this occurs in all relationships. Many of our arguments are over something equally trivial and mundane. We each refuse to do something nice for the other, often something rather insignificant and certainly nothing that would take much energy. We refuse because we are not going to be the one who is kind. Our partners do not deserve it. We deserve it. They were mean, so we're going to take our toys and go play by ourselves. We stay in our selfish, silly huff while our lives fall down around us. Remember Grandma's Maxim #68, "Two wrongs do not make a right." How much more gratifying when we make the first step towards getting that wheel going in the right direction.

My husband wants to make me happy. He's learned I'm a better person to be around when I'm happy. Aren't we all? Usually it isn't difficult to accomplish this task. I'm sincerely pleased when I see that he has done something for me that I know he didn't want to do. This usually entails doing something around the house, i.e., cleaning out the garage or fixing the gate. I once told him I worshipped the ground he worked on. I had meant to say walked on, but he thought it was more appropriate the way it had run trippingly off my tongue.

When I see how hard Leigh works, when I know he would rather be painting or creating some masterpiece, I truly appreciate what he does and I let him know how I feel. I do something considerate for him in return and so it continues. Our wheel has been going in the right direction for over thirty years, granted with a few bumps and blowouts along the way.

Many men comment that they do what makes their wives happy. "If she's not happy, I'm not happy" or "Happy wife, happy life." Leigh insists this is true and all happily married men know the wisdom inherent in these statements. He says that he has learned that if he does something I want him to do when I ask him to do it, I'm so pleased that I'm content and not complaining or nagging him until he begrudgingly concedes to my wishes. He says it's easier in the long run to just do it and doesn't know why he didn't realize this sooner in our relationship. Of course this works both ways. Isn't it easier to take a moment to do something your mate would like and enjoy the good will rather than ignoring his wishes and needs and getting the cold shoulder or the evil eye? Some people fear that if they do what their mates want them to do when they ask them to do it, the list of "Honey Do's"—"Honey do this, Honey do that"— will only grow. They fear they will do nothing else for the rest of the day or week except the "Honey Do List." If this does occur, they have a reason to resist. No one should impose a huge laundry list of demands on his mate. However, taking the time to do a task that is often simple can make a big difference in the direction of your wheel and the happiness of you and your mate.

When Words Speak Louder Than Actions

How much we care about each other is also demonstrated by what we say about each other. I sometimes compliment my husband when he is present, but frequently tell people he has never met just how wonderful he is. They're often surprised. Most people tell others the negative things about their spouses. The question arises, "Why would they stay married to such horrible people?" Even if their partners have quite a few good traits, they always seem to accentuate the negative in discussions with others. I have ceased being surprised when people whom I have never met tell me what a fantastic person I must be for my husband to say such wonderful things about me. Many times a beautiful young woman with whom my husband has been working is the bearer of this news. Leigh is a true anomaly to these women because not only does he not hit on them, he often talks about his wonderful wife and family during their conversations together. They can't believe such a man exists.

It's important to tell your mate how much you appreciate some thoughtful deed he has done or a compliment he has given you. Tell others the good things about your mate. Word often gets back to him. How much nicer when he finds out you've been complimenting him rather than complaining about him.

My husband and I also compliment each other when we are together. Many times people say nasty things about each other in the guise of teasing or just joking. This isn't a healthy habit. Making fun of someone's weak points is never funny or a good joke, especially not to the person who is being teased. Why not tease someone about what a good person he is as opposed to all the things he isn't? I love to see the look on my husband's face when I tell people what a wonderful actor he is or how well he can handle a difficult situation with the children. He knows I'm not flattering him. He knows I mean what I say. He can tell because he sees how proud I am of him.

The Loving Habit

Keeping the wheel going in the right direction is not as difficult as getting it to go forward after it has been stuck in reverse. When you begin by being aware of someone else's needs and enjoy doing kind things for him, it can become a habit.

I'm convinced that people become accustomed to anything if they do it long enough. For example. I actually like the dry hot air popcorn that tastes like cardboard. I'm used to eating it and the buttery, salted kernels are too greasy for me now. I even like almond milk after being raised in Wisconsin on the white creamy dairy variety. So why not become accustomed to being a loving partner? It's more fulfilling than being disagreeable because you feel better about yourself and you're not constantly in a battle. If you occasionally fail and do something completely selfish or mean, it is more easily forgiven if your mate is happy and not lying in wait for you to do something wrong. He doesn't get upset and you're so glad that you do something kind. The wheel goes forward once again

Rubbing Each Other the Right Way

On the other hand, getting the wheel moving forward after years of being in reverse is a definite challenge. It's a law of physics. A moving object could move forever at the same rate, in the same direction. This is called momentum. If a ball has ever hit you hard you know what momentum is. It's similar to the feeling you get when you get hit hard by a nasty argument with your mate. You can't breathe, you double up in pain and feel like vomiting, crying or both. The only thing that will stop momentum is when a new force is applied. This new force can speed up the wheel or slow it down. In physics, friction slows the wheel down. Friction is the force between two things rubbing together. In our case, rubbing each other the wrong way stops the wheel when it's going in the right direction. When it's going in the wrong direction, the friction that comes from rubbing each other the wrong way seems to make the wheel go faster and faster. Therefore, we have to come up with another type of friction: rubbing each other the right way. Just how much rubbing together is needed to slow the wheel down depends on how fast it is moving. A lot of rubbing together could actually slow the wheel down and stop it. Then you use energy to start it moving in the new direction.

I'm not sure what Isaac Newton had in mind, but I bet you could come up with all sorts of ways to rub together. We can do the obvious and rub our bodies together. We can rub each other's backs, physically and psychologically. We can rub our heads to find ways to rub our hearts together, to get them beating again.

Changing — One Stone at a Time

Getting the wheel going in the right direction is a challenge, but it is not impossible. It takes will and hard work, like most things worth having. "Where there's a will, there's a way," Grandma's Maxim #84. You must make changes. Complaining how bad it is or saying you're going to change and never changing doesn't work. That should be apparent to you if your wheel has been in reverse this long. Start doing kind things for your mate today, without expectations. Don't expect that he will be considerate to you in return. This can't be your motivation. In fact, if you have had a nasty relationship up until now, he may not notice if you do something kind. If he does notice, he may be suspicious of your motives. What is she trying to do now? What's the trap?

If you have expectations of what your mate's response should be when you start doing kind deeds and acting with love, you are in a no win situation. He will inevitably fail to live up to your expectations. You must make the changes yourself. Start changing the part of the pattern you have the ability to change. Be responsible for your side of the problem even if you feel your mate is at fault. This may take weeks or even months. "Rome was not built in a day," Grandma's Maxim #53.

Do these things now because you want to have a better relationship and you want to have the wheel going in the right direction. Expect nothing from your mate. When someone is hurt, they are wounded and will not respond immediately. Every word said in anger creates a stone. If these stones have become a mountain you can't expect the mountain to disappear by removing one rock. It must be done one stone after another. It takes patience and perseverance. You may be pleasantly surprised.

Listen To the Voice

Most arguing is over trivial issues. We don't care about a large percentage of the things we are screaming or complaining about. Even when I appear to be very angry, there's a voice I hear if I choose to listen to it. It says, "Are you really this upset? Do you care enough about this issue to sacrifice your happiness or your partner's happiness? You seem to be caught in the drama of this situation, making it much more dramatic than it needs to be."

I have finally arrived at the point where I can sometimes stop arguing in the middle of a disagreement and start laughing. I look at my husband and say, "This is silly. Do you care this much about whatever we are arguing about?" I know it's not the norm, but my husband usually agrees with me and joins in the laughter.

This takes practice. I didn't always accomplish a laughing outcome to an argument to say the least. It seemed like I needed to be mad or upset. No amount of apologies or coddling could get me out of these moods. I refused to listen to that voice and would wallow in my misery. This was my choice. To change took desire, practice and will. Actually, a lot of desire, practice and will, and I still have relapses. It's important to realize that you can change the direction of the wheel slowly, but surely, if you have the desire and will. Do so without expectations. Do so because you want to have a loving relationship and express your love to the person with whom you have chosen to spend the rest of your life.

~ When you start a relationship, get the wheel going in the right direction immediately.

~ It's much easier to maintain momentum in the right direction, so start expressing your love and doing kind things for your mate in the beginning of a relationship and do not stop.

~ Grandma was correct when she said, "You catch more flies with a spoonful of honey than with twenty cans of vinegar," Maxim #69.

~ It's rewarding to strive toward being a kind and loving person, aware of other people's needs. You feel better.

~ It takes energy, energy that is wasted, to be disagreeable. Besides, you feel miserable most of the time and are usually alone.

~ Getting the wheel going in the right direction can become a habit for both of you. The norm can be to treat each other with love.

~ Avoid blame.

~ Invest in no-fault marriage insurance.

~ Most arguments are about inconsequential things. They rarely solve anything and usually make things worse.

~ Learn to listen to your voice of objectivity.

~ Getting the wheel going in the right direction after years of being in reverse is possible.

~ You must remove the mountain, one stone at a time. It all depends on how much desire and will you have.

~ You can rub each other in all the right ways.

~ Do you want to spend the rest of your life bickering? Have the desire and will to change the direction of the wheel. Move forward to a positive, loving, rewarding relationship for both of you.

Chapter Five

WE ARE MANY PEOPLE—
EXPERIENCE ALL OF THEM

I often hear people complain about the pattern of the relationships they've had and why they've failed. They tell me they are the giver in the relationship or the facilitator or whatever noun they choose to use to express that they do all the work in their relationships. It appears that people tend to adopt roles and can't escape them. I ask people that complain about this problem if they are only givers in other aspects of their life. Aren't they a mixture of many different personalities, desires, needs, and strengths?

Many people enjoy questionnaires that determine if you are a type A personality or a type B. Are you a warm color person or are you better suited to the cool spectrum? Are you a Pisces or a Cancer? We want to define ourselves. Things will be better once we know who we are. Ah yes, this is who I am - Aries, warm-colored, type A personality.

The problem with this equation is that we are many people. We can act a certain way with one person and a different way with someone else. We are constantly surprising ourselves. One day we feel we can conquer the world and the next day we want to pull the covers over our heads and hide from that world.

I think this is great. I love how I surprise myself. I love how my husband surprises me. I love how we change roles. It's necessary and important to be different people, to express all parts of ourselves. I'm not encouraging everyone to become Sybil with multiple personalities,

I'm encouraging you and your partner to allow each other to express the many-faceted sides of your personalities.

A boyfriend once told me that I would never be happy with one man. This might have had some influence on my idea that I would never marry. Fortunately, I fell in love with my husband, a man who has so many different qualities that I'm never bored. He also keeps evolving and growing and our relationship is never static. After all, "Variety is the spice of life," Grandma's Maxim #43.

Silent Advisors

Leigh and I fulfill different roles for each other and ourselves. I know my husband will be there to help me through a dilemma. Some people do this with sage advice, physical help, or silent listening. Have you noticed that the people with the best reputations as advisors often say nothing? You tell them the problem, they listen, and you find a solution, your own solution, although you may not realize it. It's important to verbalize what you're feeling, see it in perspective, and you often discover an answer to your needs.

My grandmother was a pro at minimalist advising. Everyone thought she gave the best advice in the world. "Ask Grandma, she'll know what do to." I was present during Grandma's advice sessions. She usually said little and rarely told anyone to do x, y and z to solve a problem. She might inject an occasional "How do you feel about that?" or "What do you think you should do?" but she never told anyone exactly what to do. She would listen to people attentively and then let them find a solution for themselves, which might be the only way to really help anyone. Many therapists are paid $200 an hour for similar advice. Inevitably, everyone who consulted Grandma went away feeling great and ready to conquer the world. Even her maxims are open to your own interpretation. This method is similar to asking a question and opening up a book, such as the Bible or the I Ching, to get an answer. Ten different people with ten different problems could open the Bible to the same verse and find the help they need. They each interpret what they are reading or hearing differently and yet know the message is meant specifically for them. Things become clear. We know what we should do; we just have to reach down inside of us and find the answer. It's there.

My husband has used all of these methods to help me. He is strong and wise. There are times, however, when he's not feeling strong or wise. Then it's my turn to become the Rock of Gibraltar.

Lean on Me

Most of us want someone who is strong, someone to lean on, someone who will take care of us. We also want our independence, to do whatever we want to do. Though an apparent contradiction, you only get in trouble when you want the whole pie at once. You must be willing to give what you get. If you want to lean on someone, you must be willing to have someone lean on you. If you want freedom, you cannot enslave. As Grandma would say, "What's good for the goose is good for the gander," Maxim #29.

It doesn't have to be a big stretch for you to be the strong one in a relationship. Even if you feel like the most helpless person in the world, you know how strong you can be. You must be strong when your child has been hurt and you must take emergency action. You must be strong when a parent has died and you need to take care of everything left behind. We have many capabilities inside of us. Let them out. Be those people. It takes the pressure off your mate. He is relieved that he doesn't always have to be a certain way. You feel better because you're not repressing large parts of yourself. You both have the freedom to be the adult, the child, the clown, the sage, the loafer, the achiever.

Giving an Inch, Gaining a Mile

You know that you're able to be different types of people, but perhaps some of the roles aren't as enjoyable to you as others. My husband prefers to stay home. He has become better about this, but there was a time when he rarely went to activities outside his close surroundings. Some of our friends have been married in our home. The joke was that it was the only way to get Leigh to come to the wedding. Knowing this, I often went places alone. I would have preferred to go with Leigh, but I knew he wouldn't enjoy himself and I'd be concerned about him, so I wouldn't enjoy myself either. Instead of forcing him to go with me and being miserable or staying at home with him and regretting that I wasn't at a particular function, I chose to go alone. I came home excited to see Leigh because I had missed him and wanted to share the evening's events with him. He was delighted to have me home and enjoyed my enthusiastic descriptions of the latest social affair.

There were times, however, when Leigh did go with me and seemed to enjoy himself, or at least made me believe he did. There were also times when I stayed home from a special occasion and didn't complain about it. It's interesting to note that over the years we have evolved to the point where Leigh occasionally goes out without me because I would rather stay home. He still prefers a creative evening at home, but we certainly enjoy the other's perspective more than either of us thought we would.

I think if Leigh had never gone out with me or I had never stayed at home with him, we wouldn't have allowed a part of us to develop that is essential to becoming a complete person. Many couples stay in the same role i.e., the husband that goes to sporting events and the wife who stays home and cooks or vice versa. The next time your spouse wants to go to a football game, go along. By meeting your partner a fraction of the way and occasionally adopting roles you never thought you would adopt, you may grow to accept or even like the new role, even if it's only because it makes the person you love happy. You don't always have to do this. Try it occasionally. You may be pleasantly surprised at the results.

Routing Routines

When I was first married, I thought it wasn't a good idea to have a designated side of the bed or specific duties at home that no one else was able to do. I didn't want to get in a rut or have the relationship with my husband become a routine. I had seen people walking through life in a trance, doing the same thing everyday and I knew this wasn't for me.

After more than thirty years of marriage, I must confess that I do have a side of the bed I sleep on most often, but Leigh and I do change sides, depending on who has to get up the earliest. Leigh also tends to deal with the technical responsibilities more than I do, but I have been known to charge a battery and take a few photos. I usually get the cars serviced more than Leigh does, but he's certainly familiar with the inside of our mechanic's shop. We don't have strict patterns of behavior where one of us is the one who takes out the trash or puts away the dishes. We exchange responsibilities as well as roles.

Many times responsibilities and roles go hand in hand. Leigh and I have exchanged major roles, such as who works outside of the home and who is the primary caregiver for our two daughters. Obviously, if he's working more, I end up doing more of the daily chores that need to be done around the house. If I'm the one working, it's easier for me to pick up something we may need from town. It makes sense to be practical about your responsibilities and roles.

Some of these responsibilities may seem trivial. Often it's these trivial responsibilities that drive someone crazy and cause great harm in a relationship. If you share roles and responsibilities, these feelings of being stuck in a certain pattern are much alleviated. You don't have to do something you hate all the time; you don't have to be a certain way all the time. Anything is easier if you realize it's not forever. Hopelessness sets in when we think we will never escape a situation. When you know that you won't always have to be working at a job that you dislike, it doesn't seem unbearable. There's a light at the end of the tunnel.

When you experience all parts of your personality and share a variety of responsibilities, you become a multi-faceted individual. Too many people are confounded by the simplest of tasks once they are no longer with their partner. They don't know how to balance a checkbook or how to decorate a Christmas tree. "Jason always did that" or "Karen took care of those things." If you want to share your lives together, experience everything. Don't get stuck in your roles or patterns. Your life will be much fuller.

Try It, You Might Like It

These ideas carry over to all areas of life. When Leigh and I were first together, I was enchanted with Tiffany-style lamps and bought two for our apartment. I thought those lamps were a high point in our decorating scheme. They came with us to our home in Malibu. One evening my husband and I were sitting in our living room and his gaze fell on the brightly lit lamps. He remarked, "Those lamps are lovely. I remember disliking them when you bought them, but now I think they're beautiful." A simple comment, but a revealing one to me. I never knew he didn't like the lamps. He knew I liked them, and apparently just let it go. He isn't one to make an issue out of something that he considers inconsequential. More importantly, by not rejecting something that was not to his taste, his taste changed and grew to include new things. The lamps are a simple example, but you can imagine the results if you are receptive to things that you may at first think boring or silly or not to your liking. You may discover a new love of opera or a fulfilling charity such as building homes for the needy. Who knows? The possibilities are endless. You also allow your mate to express himself to you without the fear of negative judgment or ridicule. You experience these same feelings of freedom. Everyone wins.

When you experience all aspects of yourself and allow your mate to do the same, change doesn't become an issue or a difficult problem. Most of us have wanted to change something about ourselves and all of us have wanted to change something about our mate. The problem with change is that most people in our lives don't change because we don't allow them to change. We see them as they have always been. We expect their behavior. We don't see them as they could be, at their highest potential. Consequently they never change and we never change. When we are used to experiencing all parts of our personalities in a relationship and playing many roles, there is no pattern, no constant type of behavior. It's easier to change when there are fewer restraints and patterns to break. When your mate doesn't expect you to be a certain way, you can both be open to new experiences, or to a part of each other that you need to express. "Why would Mary decide to go to a political rally? She always stays home with the children and has never been interested in politics." These thoughts would not occur if you were accustomed to experiencing all aspects of your personality. You would know that people change and have different desires and needs at different times. This is growth. This is change. This is good.

Dealing With Destruction

Experiencing all parts of yourself should never be an excuse for acting like a jerk. Remember you are still in a relationship with someone you love. There are two of you. It's not okay to suddenly want to experience your mean, selfish, nasty persona. If you have a mean, selfish, nasty persona and must express it, put up a punching bag in the garage or run three miles, whatever is necessary. Do not criticize your mate incessantly or treat him like your servant because you're in a mood. You have a responsibility to your relationship. You must deal with destructive parts of your personality so they don't hurt you or your relationship. You know what those destructive parts are. It's not okay to have a fling or get drunk and be abusive. Get help or channel the destructive energies into something positive. It can be done. You know you can change.

~ Don't play the same role.

~ You are many people, experience them. It can be comforting to define yourself, but it is limiting.

~ Enjoy the freedom of experiencing all parts of yourself. Allow your partner the same freedom.

~ Do not expect your partner to take care of you. Take care of each other.

~ You are capable of anything. You can be strong. You can be wise.

~ Be open to new experiences.

~ You may enjoy something you never thought you would enjoy.

~ You will expand your horizons.

~ Be aware of and change limiting patterns and routines.

~ Share responsibilities. Life will be fuller and you won't be lost if you are alone. When you share responsibilities and roles, you create options for yourself and your mate.

~ Be receptive and open to your partner's tastes and ideas.

~ Change is much easier when you are accustomed to it.

~ Expressing all aspects of yourself is not an excuse to be offensive.

~ You have a responsibility to your relationship.

Chapter Six

LESSONS FROM LEIGH

I met Leigh when he was twenty years old. I had been attracted to older men and felt if I was to ever have a lasting relationship it would be with someone older and wiser than myself. Now with Leigh, I was in love with someone younger and less worldly than me. Leigh was always wise, but I felt more educated when we were first together. I was the outstanding student, the valedictorian, the honors graduate. Leigh had attended Juilliard in New York City, but was largely self-taught through his own reading, study and experience.

Leigh has never stopped growing and learning. He has developed his genius and has taught me much about all areas of life. Four of the most important lessons regarding relationships I learned from him I call:

1. Vanquishing the Green-Eyed Monster

2. In the Mood

3. Presto Chango

4. No Expectations

Vanquishing the Green-Eyed Monster

I come from a green-eyed monster family that was quite familiar with jealousy in romantic relationships. I was taught to keep up my guard, to never trust anyone. He could be cheating on you. After all, you were probably cheating on him. Most people who suffer from jealousy know how incapable they are of being faithful to their own partners. Most people who accuse their mates of cheating have probably cheated themselves. We suspect people of doing the same things we know we do ourselves. This type of person is most jealous. Another jealous type is someone who has such low self-esteem he presumes his partner is cheating, as if it were inevitable. He feels insecure in his relationship because he thinks his partner could not really love him and must be having affairs.

Jealousy occurs when you don't feel secure. People who feel deeply loved and supported by their spouse are not the ones who are likely to fly off in a jealous rage. This occurs when you've created a foundation of insecurity by playing a game of trying to get your mate's attention by making him jealous i.e., dropping hints about how attractive and interesting someone else is with the innuendo that your partner is neither. Another way to raise the green-eyed monster is by criticizing your partner so much that he believes you don't care about him. You can also do this by ignoring him, flirting with others or being absent. There are myriad ways to make people feel insecure. We have experienced many of these ways as both the giver and receiver depending on the relationship. You would think we would realize the folly of our ways, but no. Many of us are entrenched in our patterns and refuse to change them.

Don't we realize how destructive jealousy can be and what a waste of time and energy it is? Jealously is a negative in every respect. Any relationship would be seriously undermined by someone who is constantly watching your every move to the point of interpreting an innocent hello as an invitation to a secret tryst. If you're out of sight, you must be up to no good. Thus both parties end up living on pins and needles–one fearful of being unjustly accused and the other morbidly waiting to have his worst fears confirmed. You can imagine the stress and pain involved in this scenario. Many of us have lived through it or are still living it.

I had one boyfriend who was obsessively jealous. His behavior was alien to anything I'd ever experienced, so I had no idea what to do about it. He would accuse me of many things. At the time, we were both living in Hawaii. One day I decided to wait for him on the beach in front of the hotel where he was working. He was a waiter there earning money for graduate school. I was innocently reading a book and do not remember talking to anyone. Suddenly, my enraged boyfriend appeared in front of me in a flurry and screamed at me for talking to someone on the beach. He had seen me from his eagle's perch at the top of the hotel in the restaurant where he worked. I assured him he must have seen someone else or perhaps looked out the window at the moment when someone could have asked me the time. He was certain I was setting up a rendezvous for a later date and must have a secret lover. I was innocent, but there was no way I could prove this. I could not understand his rage. I finally realized what I must do about my boyfriend's obsessive jealousy. We agreed to end the relationship.

I had never suffered from obsessive jealousy, but was no stranger to the usual feelings of doubt that invade you when you are feeling less than secure about yourself. When you don't feel as attractive or as interesting or as capable or as anything, you are ripe for the seeds of jealousy to germinate and grow.

I was feeling quite ripe during the summer when my father died. I had been working on a show at Universal Studios and Leigh (we had been together a year) was doing a film in Bermuda. I rushed home to Wisconsin when I heard my father was ill and was able to be with him for a few days before he passed away. I am thankful I had that time with him, but it was very emotional and left me off-center. I called Leigh regularly because I missed him. Any time he didn't answer in his room, my helpful family would remind me that he was an actor, an actor on location, an actor on location with a beautiful co-star, and must be cheating on me. "Out of sight, out of mind," Maxim #26, although I don't remember Grandma quoting this one to me at the time, thank goodness. She wasn't one to try to make you feel worse than you already felt. The rest of my family, however, seemed to take the ball and run with it. The capper for them was one evening when Leigh had asked the desk to forward my call to his lovely co-star's room where they were rehearsing. He wanted to make sure he didn't miss a call from me and gave me no reason to be jealous. In fact, he wanted me to join him in Bermuda as soon as possible. I, on the other hand, was more than slightly doubtful about what was going on when I finally arrived in Bermuda.

I can't blame my family for this. People can say all sorts of things, but if you have vanquished the green-eyed monster, it doesn't matter. I am not saying it's easy work to accomplish this feat. It's often difficult, but if you are successful, the rewards are great. You don't doubt your partner and are secure in your relationship. I'm reminded of a remark Alan Alda's wife made when he was at his height of popularity starring in the TV comedy "MASH." His family remained in New Jersey and he had to film the television show in Los Angeles, so he was frequently away from home. An interviewer asked Alan's wife what she would say if he told her that Alan was having an affair? She responded that she would laugh. The interviewer was somewhat perplexed. Alan Alda's wife was a lovely person, but a very typical-looking woman and her husband was being fawned upon by most of the gorgeous women of Hollywood. She would just laugh? Impossible and not your typical Hollywood response. I worked on a film with Alan a short time after his wife's comment and I saw first hand why his wife said what she did and why I am sure he loved her all the more for it. She knew her situation and was secure with herself and her husband.

Arriving in Bermuda I neither knew the situation nor felt secure within myself, let alone with my boyfriend. Leigh was filming, so I was driven to the hotel and went to his room. Leigh writes beautiful poetry and I saw some pages he was working on lying on his desk. He had written lovely poems, but I found myself wondering what (or who) had inspired them. Certainly not me. Feeling morose, I decided to take a shower. I exited the bath somewhat refreshed, but definitely not looking my best in a bulky hotel bathrobe, with no makeup and tangled hair. There was a knock at the door and I opened it to see a beautiful vision sweetly inviting Leigh and me to join her for dinner. I mumbled an agreement somewhat incoherently, and closed the door, devastated. Leigh has worked with her every day! Of course she wanted us to have dinner with her. Then Leigh could see her with me and make his decision final. She must have been smirking as she gazed upon her bedraggled competition.

Leigh was still working as the dinner hour approached. A phone call from "the vision" suggested we get together anyway and Leigh could join us later. Why not? I could be brave as I faced my fate. I walked resignedly towards the guillotine doors of her room, imagining a drum roll with each step.

There she was again, "the vision," a pleasant smile inviting me in. Was she actually going to confide her indiscretions with Leigh or merely gloat knowingly?

"You're just as lovely as Leigh's described you!" she purred. This cat was cunning. But oddly enough, she sounded genuine.

"I feel like I know you so well, you must forgive me. Leigh talks about you constantly. He's missed you. He will be thrilled to see you!"

She was sweet and sincere. Leigh had told me this was her first film. She was a definite shoo-in for an Academy Award. This kid could act.

Somehow my guard began to drop and I managed to act quasi-normal as opposed to the paranoid I had become. I was biding my time until the real culprit arrived. Wouldn't he be surprised and worried when he saw us together all chummy. My mother told me about a similar scene she once performed for my father. Picture if you will, the wife and current girlfriend singing and playing the piano. Husband arrives home unaware of meeting between wronged women and walks unknowingly into the trap. "Honey, come in," my mother coos. "We have a guest for dinner."

Oh no! Was I actually repeating my mother's relationships?

A few moments later Leigh arrived. He was thrilled to see me. There were no conspiratorial looks between him and "the vision." In fact there were no looks between them at all. My guy only had eyes for me and we had a lovely evening.

I eventually told Leigh how I had felt and we discussed it at great length. Thus was the introduction to my education on living without jealousy. Even with my twisted beginnings it was a lesson relatively easy to learn. Leigh explained to me how he sincerely believes in monogamy. That is what being in a relationship is all about. If you want to be with other people, be with them, but don't be in a one-on-one relationship. Having a good relationship is being monogamous with the person you love. You can appreciate other people and enjoy their company, but that doesn't translate to jumping in bed with them. Unfortunately many people think that it does.

Leigh has many women friends; some are even ex-girlfriends. They all adore him for many reasons, but I'm sure one of those reasons is the fact that since we've been together, Leigh has never wanted to be anything more than friends with them. Women feel safe around Leigh. They know he has no sexual interest in them even though he can care about them a great deal as people. He is the type of male friend I wanted growing up, but inevitably those friendships never worked out because the men I knew at the time wanted to be more than friends.

All this is not to say that Leigh doesn't find other women sexy. He certainly does, but it doesn't mean he has to act on it. Many people don't understand this behavior. Women who are attracted to Leigh are baffled at first. Some beautiful women who are accustomed to getting what they want don't understand when Leigh isn't interested in knowing them in a more intimate way. I have had more than a few sought-after women ask me what my secret is to have a husband so devoted to me. They have never met anyone like Leigh who could resist their charms. Eventually many of these women become our friends and value the relationship Leigh and I have together as well as our friendship with them.

It didn't take me long to realize how lethal and silly jealousy is. Having a loving, monogamous partner makes it easy for me, but some people still find ways to be jealous in an ideal situation. It seems as though they can't help adding drama to their lives by imagining their partner or themselves having secret liaisons. Don't waste your energy. If you want drama, become an actor or write a book, but don't play these games. You're playing with fire.

Leigh's behavior influenced me or maybe I grew up and realized the folly of my previous ways. I'm still charmed by an interesting, attractive man, but not in the carnal sense. When did we get the idea that any person to whom we are attracted becomes someone with whom we must play a cat and mouse game that eventually leads to sleeping together? Somewhere we have confused the issues. We act like little children who want to eat all the candy in the candy shop. Inevitably we end up with a severe tummy ache.

My answer to this quandary is to enjoy all the wonderful qualitites of the people in your life. Spend marvelous times with them, love them dearly, but save that irreplaceable feeling, those truly intimate moments for that one special person with whom you have chosen to spend your life. If monogamy is difficult for you, you may be with the wrong person or maybe you have to work at it harder. It's worth the effort.

One of the greatest benefits of this kind of a relationship is that jealousy evaporates. Few people realize the joy that comes from living a jealousy-free life. I don't have those horrible gnawing feelings in my stomach. I don't secretly hate all the beautiful women in the world or think of them as competition. I have wonderful male friends that Leigh values as much as I do. We don't have to waste valuable time and energy having silly fights over silly issues.

Of course my family still doesn't understand this concept. Any time my family visits and sees a female friend who may be talking seriously with Leigh while I'm out of the room or maybe even giving him a back massage (heaven forbid!), they end up speaking to me in hushed tones. "You better keep an eye on those two," is the usual warning. It doesn't matter if they know this person is one of our oldest friends, someone we have known for twenty years and is like our sister. There is no convincing them that hanky-panky isn't on the horizon.

Due to the arduous hours I experience when I'm working on a film, I sometimes stay in town near the studio. I'm just too tired to make the long drive home and would prefer not to fall asleep while driving over the canyon roads. I stay with friends, some of whom are very attractive men. None of us make a big deal out of it. Many times our friends may not be at home, or they are asleep when I arrive. Luckily, we have informal friends. If they are home, we're glad to see each other, may chat for a moment and then I go to bed in the guest room. I know my family and some acquaintances are amazed at this situation.

Occasionally other people we meet are uneasy with our reactions to situations that might cause them to be jealous. One week, Leigh was the guest star on a popular television show and had a kissing scene with the leading lady whom we had never met. I was there for the rehearsal and afterwards Leigh came over to the audience section where I was sitting and spoke with me. When he returned to the set, the leading lady looked at him guiltily and asked, "Was your wife upset? What did she say to you?" Leigh assured her, "Carla was telling me that I should kiss you more passionately in the last scene. She didn't think it was convincing."

Of course the actress was surprised, but I'm sure much more relaxed. I don't mean to suggest that I would coach my husband on lovemaking in a real situation, but being in the film business I know how awkward these scenes are and just how unromantic they can be. Besides, I didn't think they had kissed passionately enough for the scene and I want my husband to do the best job he can do.

I realize that I'm making the idea of living without jealousy sound simple. I'm sure many of you think it would be impossible to do. I assure you it is not. I can't promise that it will be easy for all of you, but I do know that it isn't impossible. It's worth every effort to become free of the green-eyed monster. When I was faced with a dilemma, Grandma would often remind me, "A problem is a chance for you to do your best," Maxim #70. If jealousy is a problem, do your best now. Some things I would suggest are:

1. Stop living the life of a drama queen. It seems that many people need to have conflict and emotional outbursts and even self-imposed misery to feel alive. Everything is a soap opera for them: I'm the victim; I'm unloved; I'm misunderstood; I can't help myself.

They are wrong. They can stop. Extricating yourself from these tangled webs is difficult, but you can begin by listening to that voice of reason we all have. You may have become so capable of acting distraught that you believe you are distraught. Realize that if you keep creating all these dramatic scenarios for yourself, you're going to be miserable and alone. Don't play games that only end up hurting you and others. You don't want to make your partner jealous just to see how much he cares about you. You should know how much he cares about you and if you don't, you better have a serious talk with him and find out. You solve problems by communicating with your partner as an honest, supportive adult. You will never find any answers or solve any problems by acting upset, jealous, hurt, or over-reacting. Stop acting! Do not be a drama junky. Do something creative with that energy. Join a theater group or write poetry. Be honest in your relationships.

2. Use self-discipline. Realize what is important to you. Is a quick fling really worth destroying your marriage, your children, your partner, yourself? A relationship is like a boat. Even if it is a giant luxury liner or an indestructible battleship, you poke enough holes in it, it's going to sink. Keep your relationship sound. Think of it as a third entity. You, your partner and your relationship. Do what is good for all of you. You'll have more profound relationships with people when you can appreciate their minds and souls without feeling the necessity to jump in bed with them. Respect other people, respect yourself. Have your intimate relationship, the most extraordinary one you could possibly have, with your partner.

3. Prioritize. As we have heard many times, no one ever said, "I wish I could have spent more time at the office," on his deathbed. Spend time with your loved one. Leigh and I have prioritized our time with each other and our two daughters. We love the rest of our family and our friends, our work, our creative pursuits, but our time together comes first. It would be difficult not to rile the green-eyed monster if you spend your free time with your new friend even if you are monogamous and it's a strictly platonic relationship. You must take care of your garden or weeds grow, the soil dries out and all your beautiful plants die. Leigh and I tend to spend time together with our friends, as they are primarily mutual friends. But that isn't always the case. We each spend time alone

with friends and family. However, both of us know that when we all have such little time, our first priority is to be together.

4. Have self-confidence. Don't doubt yourself and think you are less than you are. When your partner compliments you, trust that he is sincere. You're worth compliments and more. You deserve your mate's love and affection. I know this self-confidence is a challenge. Sometimes, it evaporates at crucial moments. I have many lapses myself. I've noticed this recently as I get older. I remember Grandma's Maxim #72, "Wrinkles merely indicate where smiles have been," but even so, there are times when I think I'm not as attractive as I used to be and a doubt may creep in. Does he think I am less attractive? My husband expresses himself easily with compliments, but he isn't always there to say the right words. At those times I re-evaluate myself and realize there may be a few more wrinkles on my face, but I'm more interesting and wiser. I also contemplate changes I can make. I can exercise more, watch my diet more carefully, try a new lipstick or hairstyle, do a few facial exercises or read an interesting book. It never hurts to make the most of what nature has provided.

In the Mood

It hasn't been a great day. You're feeling depressed, angry, and unfulfilled. Your unsuspecting mate comes home, makes an innocent comment, and you're ready for WWIII. Unless you have a mate who takes cover until the attack passes or he decides to go AWOL, WWIII might occur. We've all been here, in the grips of such moods. When these moods fell upon me, I felt that I was helpless and there was nothing to be done. Even Grandma's Maxim #74, "At least when you are down you don't have to worry about falling," could not cheer me.

I was going to be inconsolable until the mood decided it would take its leave of me. The mood had all the control; I had none. No one else had any control either. I couldn't be talked out of my mood, caressed out of it, laughed out of it - nothing. I was it until "it" passed.

Then along came Leigh. He said a very simple thing. "You have the ability to change your mood." My immediate response was that this guy didn't know what it was like to be a woman in the grips of a powerful emotion. There was no way I could change the way I was feeling. I was certain I had tried and never succeeded. Leigh continued to weather quite a few outbursts and always said the same thing. "You are in control. You can change your mood."

It took me a few years to follow his wisdom, but I finally came to the conclusion that he is absolutely correct. He never gave me any helpful hints on how to change my mood, all he did when I was seemingly consumed by a certain emotion was repeat the same phrase, "You are in control. You can change your mood." Maybe it became a mantra that finally sunk in. I really don't know how it happened, but thankfully it did. This knowledge gave me the freedom to decide my own fate in a situation. It didn't stop me from becoming depressed or angry or frustrated, it gave me the ability to stop feeling depressed or angry or frustrated. I realized that I had to deal with whatever problem existed, but I was no longer a victim of my own emotions. This knowledge allowed me to discuss problems and solve them rationally, feel happier and be someone with whom my family wants to spend time.

The biggest step in developing this ability is to realize that you already have it. Grandma had a similar idea when she said, "When God gives you lemons, make lemonade," Maxim #73. You can turn those lemons into something sweet and refreshing. Everyone gets upset at some point, but knowing you do not have to keep feeling upset and miserable is liberating. You can experience a more positive mood and deal with whatever you have to deal with without having your face twisting in anger, your stomach churning and your voice squealing.

It is similar to that inner/outer voice I've talked about before. Many times I heard the voice saying, "Do you really feel this bad? Aren't you overreacting just a tad?" but I disregarded it. If I did acknowledge it, I might realize it was right, but I never thought I could do something about it, that I could take a deep breath and decide to be strong or happy or kind. It was my choice and with practice, possible to do.

Leigh set an example for me. He could become upset and angry, but he never seemed to be engulfed in these emotions. He certainly never carried a grudge. I could see how he changed his mood. He didn't avoid the problem; he simply changed how he felt as he dealt with the problem or realized there really wasn't that much of a problem. When we look at something rationally, the proportion and magnitude of a concern greatly diminishes.

Our children have grown up with this self-empowering knowledge. Whenever they were pouting or being mean or feeling upset, Leigh would take them aside and talk to them. He said many things, but the common theme was that they had the power to change how they felt and how they behaved toward others. They could be kind or mean. They could stay angry or they could decide to have a more positive attitude. Every time (and I am not exaggerating) the girls would emerge from these conversations with their father, they would be changed for the better. They would go into our room or their room in tears or angry and come out laughing and smiling. I could not believe how they were transformed. I often listened to hear what Leigh did behind closed doors. Was he bribing them? I never heard everything he said, nor have I developed this talent to the degree that he has, but his general theme was that we all have control to choose how we react to something. We are not victims. This advice was given sternly at first, then with more affection and as the girls' mood changed, with laughter and tickles.

You are in control. You can change your mood. Keep saying this. Keep hearing this. Keep acting on this. It works.

Presto Chango

It is the holiday season. Your family is gathering for the traditional holiday meal. If you are lucky this can be a joyous time. If you are like most people, this can be a stressful time. You know you will have to endure each family member's eccentric behavior that invariably seems to end in an argument with mean words and tearful exchanges. It's always the same. Your family never changes. Your brother is still the same holier than thou bigot. Your sister is still complaining about not being understood. Your brother-in-law is still petty and critical. You know them from years of experience and they never change. You know exactly how they will be and of course they live up to all your expectations.

Consider going to the holiday celebration with all your memory of each person in your family erased. You are a victim of amnesia and approach the gathering with no idea of how anyone will be. You see your family as people you are meeting for the first time. You are taking the first step towards allowing them to change.

As I mentioned before, many of us complain about how our family or our partners never change. We know all their negatives and we can never see beyond them. I am proposing that because of this strong negative memory we have of those closest to us, we never allow those we wish would change to change.

When I feel I have made some great positive stride in my life, I get a call or a visit from a member of my family. I may feel I have become a new person, but somehow, they seem to push all the buttons and my "new person" evaporates. The fates challenge us in the most powerful way, "So you think you've changed. Wait until we finish with you." You are put through the ultimate test before you have consolidated your forces. It is an evil trick the universe plays on you and you fail miserably, but you inevitably try again, just like all of us who are trying to evolve. We know from experience that change is an ongoing process, sometimes in the two steps forward, one step back tradition. We also know "You miss 100 per cent of the shots you never take," Grandma's Maxim #75. We meet some challenges successfully and others, well, better luck next time.

Your partner or family member is not going to allow you to make that change in your life easily because he sees you from his memory. You are a certain way and that is the way you will remain for him until at last he is able to see you differently. He is doing to you exactly what you do to him. This behavior is not meant in a grievous manner, it's just what most people do. We must get past this and see people in the present to allow them to change, otherwise we will file them away in the same cabinet that we have made for them. They will continuously live down to our expectations.

This isn't an easy thing to do. I haven't perfected it. I wasn't even aware of it until Leigh pointed it out to me. One day after a typically frustrating call from a family member, I was complaining about how she never changes and I wished she would. He questioned my wish.

"Do you really want this person to change?" he asked.

"Of course I do," I responded.

"Allow her to change then. Give her permission. Stop seeing her from your memory. You two rarely see each other and don't know much about each other's daily lives. I'm sure you both are different from the image you have of one another. You fall into old patterns with each other. You end up acting and reacting in the same old ways because you see each other in the same old ways. Start seeing this person in a new light. Notice all the positive things she does that are different. Do not react the same way you have been reacting. Allow her to change."

I knew what Leigh was saying was right. I just wasn't sure how to stop viewing this family member from my memory. At first I decided to react differently to what she would say or do. This was a good start. When she told me her problems I didn't give her advice as I usually did. This helped because I didn't feel frustrated with all her excuses about why she couldn't do something and I didn't feel like I was wasting my time trying to help someone who didn't want to help herself. It helped her because she didn't have to justify her behavior to me; she didn't have to feel less than me. I wasn't judging her or telling her what to fix. I didn't automatically see what she was doing as the same thing she had done before. I didn't play out the whole scenario in my head before it occurred. I didn't expect that she would bring up the same comments she always brought up about me that elicited the same reaction from me. I stopped the whole chain reaction by reacting differently, changing a simple behavioral pattern I had with her. Guess what? She was different. I had boxed her into her behavior patterns with me because I was willing to play out the other side of the scenario. By not falling into that pattern, I allowed her to react as she would with someone new who had no preconceived ideas about her. I allowed her to change.

I am still not always successful at Presto Chango. It takes conscious work and I get lazy. It is difficult not to have certain ideas about people, to interpret what they are saying as if they had an agenda or ulterior motive. We believe we know what and who they are. We assume for them. I was once told by a successful producer, "Never assume. It only makes an 'ass' out of 'u' and 'me'." It is certainly true here. When we assume people's motives, our reaction to them disallows any change they might have made.

Our interpretations are a shorthand that we use too often. When someone enters a room and says, "I'm a Democrat," we all respond, "Hmmm. Ah yes." As if that really means something. Why do we ask people what they do or what their sign is? We want that shorthand interpretation to file everyone away. It is meaningless, yet we continue to do it.

One person who comes to our discussion groups remarked, "Do you realize that I have been coming to these groups for months and I know everyone's name, but I have no idea what they do for a living, whether they are rich or poor, or what their social status might be." We both agreed that this was refreshing. In the groups, people discuss ideas and no one gives more credence to someone's ideas because of who he or she is. Very few people know anything about the other's external trappings and could care less.

In your relationships allow people to change. See them in a new light without your history together. React differently to them. Do not interpret what they really mean, who they really are or think they have an agenda. Even if they do have an agenda, if you don't react in the expected way, you may change it. Old patterns can change. People can change. You can change. Presto Chango.

No Expectations

As Grandma used to say, "If you expect nothing, you will never be disappointed," Maxim #55. My interpretation of this was that if you didn't have high expectations or goals for yourself, you would end up with nothing and be nothing. One must expect the most of oneself or suffer the consequences. Grandma used to chide me with this occasionally if I became idle and wasn't practicing the piano or doing my lessons. One must aim high in this world. You get what you put into a situation.

Leigh made me see this saying in a different light, one that has worked well in our relationship and our relationships with friends and family. He often says he expects nothing from his friends. This may sound odd, but it is admirable. What Leigh means is that he isn't in a relationship with people to get something from them. He doesn't expect their help. He doesn't expect them to call him. He doesn't expect them to give him a birthday present or thank him if he gives them one. He doesn't expect them to pick him up from the airport or take care of our dogs. He doesn't expect them to loan him money or compliment him.

Because he expects nothing from anyone, Leigh is never disappointed by anyone. He doesn't suffer from hurt feelings. He doesn't feel betrayed or ignored by anyone. This doesn't mean that he isn't happy when people do wonderful things. He is self-sufficient, but he is appreciative and honored by people's kind and considerate actions toward him. He just doesn't expect these actions or feel they are his due. Leigh has a wonderful group of friends and family who I know would do anything for him. He has never made an issue of how he feels, but it is interesting how it makes a difference in his relationships. People are free around him.

How many of us get upset because a friend didn't call us or a nephew didn't write us a thankyou note for a present we had given him? How many of us have been on the receiving end of the cold chill because our brother felt we slighted him in some way or because we did not acknowledge our spouse on our anniversary? Do you realize how freeing it is to not feel these emotions of hurt pride or guilt? Leigh's motto is, "If you don't feel like doing something for someone, don't do it. If you do, do it only because you want to and don't expect a thank you or a similar action in return." This is the true spirit of giving, but one most of us have not achieved.

Many people only give to be thanked or elicit behavior they want from others by making them feel guilty. They feel they're owed respect or attention from others. They expect their spouse to behave a specific way towards them. Anything less than this behavior is considered betrayal. "If you don't do this for me, you must not really love me" — the ultimate complaint of a spoiled child. People who must be around them feel uncomfortable. They might break the rules or offend them in some way without realizing it. It is difficult to live with someone when you are on a credit/debit account. I have known such people and would prefer they never gave me anything or did anything for me. I don't want to be constantly reminded of how much they have done for me or what I owe them.

Don't misunderstand me. I believe in manners. Grandma always told me, "Manners are the grease that keeps the wheel of civilization turning," Maxim #16. It is important to be courteous to people, to write thank you notes and to have the words "Please" and "Thank you" be an integral part of one's vocabulary. In short, to always practice the golden rule, "Do unto others as you would have them do unto you," Grandma's (and what should be everyone else's) Maxim #1. I try to raise my children with these values and make sure they understand the responsibility they have to be decent and kind people. They know certain types of behavior are unacceptable. It is my duty as a parent to put them through this training school so they can live well and pass on the legacy to their children. I don't teach them to be kind to someone just because that person will then be pleasant to them or give them a present. They know that many times people do not reciprocate when you're generous with them. You're compassionate to them because that is your nature. There are no ulterior motives. There are no expectations. You do the right thing. You do it because it's a part of you and that's what you do.

~ The lessons I've learned from Leigh have become an integral part of my life. I haven't yet mastered them. Every day I must keep working on them, but they do start to become second nature after much practice.

~ You learn you can work to vanquish the green-eyed monster of jealousy, be in any mood you choose, allow people and yourself to change, and do the right thing without expectations from other people.

~ You know that by doing these things you become a better person. You are also a happier person. You are capable of anything.

~ None of these lessons are impossible to learn.

~ As Grandma used to say, "Do not put off until tomorrow what you can do today," Maxim #4.

~ Start learning Leigh's lessons today. They will make your tomorrows better.

Chapter Seven

LET'S GET TOGETHER

We all know Grandma's Maxim #19, "Absence makes the heart grow fonder." There is no doubt that after being away from someone you love, you can't wait to see him. Your heart starts to pound faster at the thought of being together again. Your passion is at its peak. Many couples yearn for these moments. They enjoy being apart just so they can come back together again and experience that heightened intensity of emotion.

This may work well for couples on the short term. I'm not against short separations from a loved one. You don't have to always be together. There are times when Leigh needs to have solitude and escape the everyday trappings that no one wants to deal with. It's easy to get bogged down by all the "stuff" and never get anything of importance accomplished. Leigh needs solitude to think, to paint, and to write. I recognize this and try to help him by taking on more of the responsibilities that we usually share. Leigh does the same for me. I also need to have some solitude, as we all do. When my family has not been able to accompany me somewhere, I have traveled without them. I am excited to see them when I return. I also come back inspired from the experience of being away. However, another of Grandma's Maxims, #26, "Out of sight, out of mind," can also be true.

Tending Your Garden

Leigh and I are both in the film business. Sometimes our jobs require us to go on location for a few days or several months. From the very beginning of our relationship we decided that we would not allow ourselves to be separated for any length of time that could be detrimental to our family or to each other. We realized our relationship was like a beautiful garden that must be tended to flourish. It is difficult to do so when you are not together. We have remained true to our decision and it has affected us positively. We have turned down jobs that would have required us to be apart for too long or we have accepted them and gone together. We aren't insecure in our ability to withstand such separations nor do we doubt each other's fidelity. However, we've both seen too many long distance relationships falter and die. Living separate lives for long periods of time isn't good for any relationship, no matter how strong it is. If you have chosen to share your life with someone, share it. Make whatever sacrifices you must make. The most important thing you have in this life is your life together. Cherish it. Protect it.

Leigh and I met while working together and even though our jobs are different, we have the advantage of a shared interest in our work. When we go on location it's a good experience for both of us. We are together, doing what we love, with the added benefit of travel. It's not only healthy for our relationship, it also makes us happier in our work and we do a better job. Missing each other and not sharing our experiences doesn't distract us. We can help each other in our professions in many ways by taking care of something necessary the other might not have the time to do and give each other support. Our work improves as well. Even if you and your mate don't share similar professions, you can still work better together, as opposed to being apart. Being together is worth any sacrifices you may have to make.

One of our closest friends, Casey, is an actor. He never wanted to settle down, so his gypsy lifestyle of touring theatre companies and film locations suited him and he seemed content. Casey finally met the woman of his dreams and was willing to do anything to make this relationship work. He was in love and had a fairytale courtship and marriage. He was ready to settle down and tend to his garden.

Casey's wife was a working actress as well. They both received offers to work in different places at different times. They chose to take the offers and to live apart many months of the year. Their visits and reunions were marked with unbridled passion and their marriage appeared to go well—for two years. This wasn't a passing fancy for either of them. They were a truly committed couple that could have had a great future together. Unfortunately, their relationship began to falter and crack and finally ended in a huge and bitter breakup. Ten years later our dear friend was still lamenting the end of his perfect marriage. He didn't bemoan its death verbally, constantly living in the past. He rarely discussed it. Casey knew and we knew that he and his wife had made a big mistake, one that could have been avoided if they had made different choices in their careers.

You could say that this marriage would have ended anyway if it couldn't withstand the pressures of being apart. People must pursue their dreams and know they gave their all to be a success in their chosen career. That's what Casey and his wife did and the sacrificial lamb was their relationship. The sacrificial lamb will always be your relationship with your spouse or with your children. You can't be together when you're apart. These are the rules and you must play by them if you want a successful relationship.

You don't have to give up your careers either. It's a matter of priorities. You make the necessary adjustments. Casey and his wife could have tried to work in the same location or they could have alternated with one sacrificing his job one time and the other doing it the next time. People can be very creative with their work if they try. You just have to make the decision to put your relationship first.

There is sometimes a problem with time spent on activities other than careers. If your wife decides to go on a mountain climbing expedition for three months or your husband wants to join an ashram for a year, reconsider your life together. If you value your relationship, go together or come to a mutual agreement as to who will go where for two weeks or do something that will fulfill their needs at home. It's important that you both realize how necessary it is to be together. If one of you doesn't care about it, you have a serious problem. No matter how strong your relationship appears to be, you will inevitably grow apart. A life not shared is just that.

My friend, Rachel, met a young man, Greg, when she attended the University of California in Santa Barbara for a summer session. They became close and she was sure Greg was the man she wanted to marry. In autumn, Rachel went back to school at Dartmouth and Greg continued at Santa Barbara. They maintained their relationship and kept their plans for marrying even though they were separated for long periods of time. They saw each other whenever they could and kept in touch via telephone, email, and letters, but I marveled that they still were in love after being apart a majority of the three years they were together. Rachel told me when she made up her mind about someone, it was for life. I was happy for them and knew their relationship must be very strong.

After they both graduated, Rachel continued with her plans to go to graduate school, probably in New York. Greg was planning on staying in California and becoming a chiropractor. Greg wanted Rachel to come to California. She didn't realize how important it was for their relationship that she go to California and didn't make plans to do so. Today Greg lives in California, is a chiropractor and is married. Rachel lives in New York and has a good job with an investment firm. I know a compromise of some sort could have been worked out and that these two could be together today. Rachel realizes she forgot to tend her garden. It went too long without care and all the flowers wilted and died. She thought the garden would always be there because she would always be there to smell the roses. Greg got tired of waiting to have a life together. They ended up not being together because they had been apart too long.

Living Apart Together

Of course you can be apart even when you are physically together. If one of you is working or playing all the time and you never see each other, the other might as well be on location. No matter what you're doing, if you end up being apart a majority of the time, make the necessary changes now to be together more. The money you are earning or the sacrifices you are making for each other will not be worth anything when you wake up and are no longer with the person you love or you no longer love the person you are with. Either way, you both lose.

I work in a business where sixteen-hour days can be the norm. People often bring pictures to work for others to see their beautiful new home or their daughter's graduation. I often think they bring the pictures more for themselves, just to see what they have worked for all these years. They spend their lives away from their families giving them all the good things, but before they know it, their lives and their families have slipped away. The divorce rate is high and most relationships tend to fail. Yet most of the people continue to work show after show with no time off to enjoy the fruits of their labor. They have forgotten to set priorities that could have made their lives much richer than all the money they have earned. Sadly, they now can spend their money on alimony.

The Important Experience Experienced Together

Getting together is important in any relationship. Children suffer when neither parent is with them. Parents decide that they both must work all the time to give their children a better life. The better life ends up with the children resenting their parents' absence and having serious emotional problems that are difficult for both parents and children.

As I previously mentioned, when Leigh or I go on location, we both go. Since we have had children we all go. Many people say they can't accompany their spouses when they have to travel. The usual reason is that it would be too hard on the children. I think it's too hard on the children if they don't go. I could not imagine one of us being away from our girls for a month or more. But how can they miss school? Their social lives will be in upheaval. Both of our children are honor students, popular and well-adapted. Traveling has only added to their lives. Your children can attend school wherever the family goes or be home-schooled while they are away. I've found travel to be an education in itself. Children learn an enormous amount with that stimulation alone and seem to become more socially adaptable with travel. They meet fascinating people and have interesting conversations about their new experiences. Our youngest daughter, Brighton, seems to adopt elderly women on our sojourns and has a grandmother in many places around the world. The girls have always enjoyed themselves when we have had to travel and they are also happy to come home again. The important part of the experience is that we experienced it together.

In With the Good, Out With the Bad

When I was a child, my mother would give me a big hug whenever she felt I needed one or I told her I needed one. As she hugged me, she would say, "In with the good," as we both inhaled deeply, and "out with the bad," as she squeezed me tightly and we both exhaled completely. I would feel much better after these hug fests and highly recommend them. I continue the tradition with my own children. Hugging is positive therapy for anyone. Think how much better an elderly person would feel if he received some hugs now and then. Even people who are uptight when you first put your arms around them somehow seem to melt if you do it often enough or long enough.

Spooning for Life

I told Leigh about the positive effects hug therapy has on me and he has taken over as my hug dispenser. Leigh's energy does much the same for me that mine does for him. I can feel tension literally melt away just by touching each other. We enjoy that wonderful position called spooning. We fit together like two spoons, body completely touching body. It doesn't matter who's in front or who's in back. We can alternate. I have a sensation of actually melting into Leigh. The energy exchange is felt throughout the entire body, which is a wonderful experience. Try it. I guarantee you'll like it and become spooners for life.

Pictured left and above:
Grandma Mary and Carla

Mom and Dad

Pictured above and right:
The Three Sisters
(Shortly after moving to
Grandma's house):
Lynne-10, Cheryl-8 and Carla-2

Family photo B.C. (Before Carla)
Back Row: *Father Don Reinke,*
Uncle Frederick B. Steele
and Aunt Loraine Steele
Front Row: *Sister Lynne,*
Grandmother Mary V. Steele,
Cousin John Steele, Sister Cheryl,
Mother JoAnn,
Grandfather Clarence B. Steele

Leigh's first Head Shot

Leigh's Juilliard Student ID

Right: *Publicity photos from Leigh's first television movie,* **Dawn: Portrait of a Teenage Runaway,** *with Eve Plumb*

Leigh also starred in the sequel, **Alexander: The Other Side of Dawn.** *Both were the highest rated TV films of their time*

Leigh's first television show, **Phyllis,** *starring Cloris Leachman in the title role*

*Above and Right: Stills from **Executive Suite**, the show where Carla and Leigh met. A bare-chested Leigh shooting a scene at Paradise Cove and Leigh and Brenda Sykes—one of the first inter-racial couples on prime time television.*

*Leigh as Tieran on **Star Trek Voyager***

*Leigh as Kevin from **Just One of the Guys***

*Still shot from the film **Fraternity Vacation.** Leigh portrayed Chas Lawlor*

98

*Leigh on an episode of **Paper Chase**, "The Man in the Chair"*

Various shots of Leigh in magazines from *Vogue* to *Playgirl*
(Sorry ladies—only fully clothed shots were taken)

Leigh and Carla's Wedding

*Carla in **School for Wives***

*Carla's Wedding as Emily in **Our Town***

*Leigh and Charlene Tilton in "Wedding of the Year" on **Dallas**. That episode was watched by hundreds of millions of viewers*

*Leigh and Cindy Grover in **Married: The First Year**— Leigh was filming this television series when he and Carla were married*

100

Various Shots of Leigh and Carla During *Dallas* Years

LEIGH McCLOSKEY
Can He Stand Up To J.R. and Bobby?

LEIGH McCLOSKEY: CAN HE STAND UP TO J.R. AND BOBBY?

ABOVE: Handsome Dallas star Leigh McClosky hides some good looks behind a beard as he parties with wife Carla.

DALLAS STARS COME OUT TO PAY A SAD FAREWELL

Leigh McCloskey was in a somber mood and his wife Carla was clearly upset.

Blanche Davis, the actor's widow, fights back the tears as an usher comforts her.

Leigh and Carla at Zuma Beach (photo by Herb Ritz)

Leigh and Carla—True flower children

Carla and Caytlyn—Adapting to a new life

*Leigh and Chester the chinchilla—
Carla knew Leigh would be a good father
after seeing him with Chester*

Leigh was a spokesperson for Max Factor's
California for Men

The McCloskey Family on location in Alabama

My Knight in Shining Armor
*Leigh in **Hearts in Armor***
filmed on location in Italy

Leigh and Ronn Moss,
one of our dearest friends
*on set of **Hearts in Armor***

Other Location Films

Leigh starring as
Magnus in
***Bermuda Depths**.*
The film is a
cult favorite

***Bermuda Depths**—*
Spanish Poster

***Bermuda Depths** was filmed on location*
in Bermuda and debuted on ABC

Leigh starred in
***Inferno**,*
a film by
Dario Argento
shot in Rome

Some of Leigh's Soap Opera Roles

Zack Kelton on **Santa Barbara**

Ethan Asher on **Santa Barbara**

Doctor Baranski
on **General Hospital**

Damian Smith
on **General Hospital**

Drake on **One Life to Live**

Kurt Kostner on **Young and the Restless**

A Few of the Other Women in Leigh's Life

Leigh with Lucy–Lynn Herring
General Hospital

Leigh with Bobbie–Jackie Zeman
General Hospital

Leigh with Katherine–Mary Beth Evans
General Hospital

Leigh with Laura–Christopher Norris
Santa Barbara

Leigh with Sydney Coleman
Young and the Restless

*Leigh with
Charlene Tilton
Dallas*

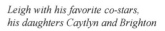
Leigh with his favorite co-stars,
his daughters Caytlyn and Brighton

Leigh and Carla at an opening gala

The Girls on Location—A balancing act,
but ultimately you learn to dance

Leigh and Carla working together on **Babylon 5** with
Tony Dow. Leigh protrayed Thomas (in *Phoenix Rising*
and *A Tragedy of Telepaths)*

Leigh appeared in **Deep Space Nine** as Joran Belar

Carla tending her garden

Carla and Leigh at home
in their garden

Leigh in the studio
with some of his paintings

Exchanging Energy

There are times when being together is not just a good idea, but an absolute necessity for Leigh and me. I'm not talking about what most people consider making love, I'm talking about just physically touching one another. Obviously touching is a part of making love, but this need is one of being in physical contact. Our bodies seem to have an electrical charge for one another and we need to physically transmit that energy by touching. I can tell when Leigh's energy is bouncing off the wall, so to speak. He is usually stressed and when I touch him his energy feels chaotic. This is something to which you can become attuned. Touch your partner. You can feel how they feel. They may feel calm and soothing or frantic and confused. They could be experiencing a multitude of emotions. When Leigh's energy is chaotic, I can ground him with my energy by lying next to him, enveloping him. I can feel the energy flow between us. I can feel my energy neutralizing his chaotic or negative energy. I do this energy exchange consciously and from an early experience we had together I believe it's the best way to do it.

Once, when we were asleep, Leigh awakened in a disturbed state. He put his arms around me and felt this wonderful exchange of energy. I slept through the whole experience, but awakened an hour later feeling as if I had a huge weight on my chest and barely able to breathe. Leigh took me to the emergency room. I was gasping for breath the entire time, but eventually returned to normal. I had no idea what had occurred. Leigh was, understandably, completely unnerved. He believed he had caused my attack. He had no idea his negative energy would affect me the way it had. He explained what had happened to me and said that he could not allow himself to touch me again if he was in such an agitated state. Once I understood what had happened, I believed that it had occurred only because I was not aware it was happening. I was asleep and may have been far away from my body, therefore my body did not know what to do with the frenetic energy that was suddenly merging with it. I had no fear this incident would repeat itself when I was awake and it never has.

There are times when Leigh says, "I don't think I should hold you right now. I'm afraid you could absorb too much of my negative energy." I reassure him that by touching each other it will only help him and I'm protected from any of the negativity he is experiencing. I can eliminate his negative energy and prevent it from affecting me by allowing it to flow through me and be released.

~ Touching your partner and feeling their energy, calming them with your own hug therapy, and spooning are great for any relationship.

~ Being together is essential for couples. Time apart can take its toll on any relationship.

~ A beautiful garden needs much of your time.

~ You must decide how you want to live your life with the person you love.

~ You can make excuses and say that life has set its course for you to follow and you have no choices or you can set your own course for your life and know what you are willing to do.

~ When you set priorities, life seems to fall into place.

~ You must realize you and your partner do not have to live your lives in the conventional manner.

~ Do things the way they work best for both of you and your relationship.

~ There are times when you will think something is impossible, but if you make priorities, life finds a way.

~ Make being together your priority. Your garden will flourish and grow.

Chapter Eight

GROWING TOGETHER AND APART

Growth is an essential part of any relationship. If you do not grow you stagnate and die. This is a rule of nature. When growth stops, deterioration and eventually death occur. Things change and go through cycles, according to Pete Seeger, The Byrds, the Bible and Grandma, "To everything there is a season, and a time to every purpose," Maxim #65. This was obvious growing up in the Midwest where I could see the changes brought by every season. I eagerly awaited them all. The first fragrance of spring, clean and fresh, greeting you as you walk out your door, a welcoming sign that the long winter is finally over. The warm summer sunshine toasting your bare shoulders as you rock back and forth on the front porch swing peering up into the treetops, watching the merry antics of the squirrels. The glorious reds, oranges and yellows of the trees and the whiff of bonfires herald the autumn chill. The stillness and beauty of the first snowfall brings wonder on a star-filled winter night. There were always these changes in the seasons of my life. I was born with change and have welcomed it.

Relationships and people go through similar changes. They all have their seasons. They go through cycles and growth. In a relationship we begin with horns and whistles celebrating everything that is exciting and new and wonderful. Things settle down somewhere along the line, depending on the people involved, but after a few days, weeks, months, years or decades we may stop seeing our relationship through rose-colored glasses and take a hard look at reality, which may show us a very different picture. This does not have to be a negative picture. Spring and autumn are different, but one is not better than the other. Though you may prefer one to the other, each has its favorable factors and fans. The change in your relationship may just take some adjustment or growth for both of you.

Looking back on over thirty years spent together, I have enjoyed each phase of Leigh and my relationship. It has been similar to watching our children grow. Each new year seemed to be better than the last. I often tell new parents, "If you think three is a great age, wait until you experience four." Children are constantly unfolding, emerging. There are always those terrible twos or the problems of puberty for you and your child, but even those times are generally remembered with more joy than sorrow. You experience and make adjustments to deal with all the ages and you change as you make those adjustments. The cycles spiral on and on. Changes in your relationship mold new parts of yourself or perhaps bring out characteristics that may have been lying dormant. You make the necessary changes. You grow as your relationship grows.

Skipping Steps Does Not Work

Today, when everyone is craving an instant relationship, people want to skip steps and phases. The courting ritual is most often complained about, especially from people in their thirties and beyond. My girlfriends, who find themselves dating again after many years in a relationship, don't want to go through the process of getting to know someone. They want to know someone immediately. "Is this guy going to be a good relationship prospect or will I be wasting my time? I don't have the time to waste and I want to know now." That is why many men and women develop the instant resume. This is who I am, this is my history, here are my goals in twenty-five words or less.

My friend, Ann, has gone through the dating ritual so often that she has edited many parts of her resume. She now believes she has a very streamlined version where she can present herself and get most of the information she needs from a date in less than an hour. Ann is still dating. Unfortunately for her, you cannot get to know someone with words describing who you are, what you have been, and where you are going. You must spend time with each other and experience these things. A relationship, like a seed, can only germinate and grow if you give it the right mixture of nutrients. Grandma knew this very well, "Time tells all," Maxim #36. Only through time can you determine if you are able to have a good relationship with someone. Once you determine this, it is only through time that you can grow together and have your relationship grow stronger, deeper.

Or not. Problems tend to arise when you don't grow along with each other or the relationship. We have all heard the complaint, "We grew apart." It's one of the most common reasons given for a failed relationship. Sometimes people get lazy to the point that they no longer sense how their partner is growing or times are changing. They stay at square one and do not move forward. Square one is comfortable, we know it. It becomes easy and rote. It doesn't challenge us.

It may work to stay at square one if your partner stays there and you both are happy there. Square one to me may be square one hundred and one to someone else. "To each his own," Grandma's Maxim #41. If it works, great. "If it's not broken, don't fix it," Maxim #56 also applies. The only problem is when we are on completely different squares and maybe not even in the same game.

Growing in Different Directions

Couples don't have to grow in exactly the same way together. Leigh is a bibliophile and has a tremendous book collection. I have an enormous love for books as well. I love to touch them, to smell them, and yes, to read them. Leigh has taken my love of books and expanded it one hundred fold. His interest in them, especially antiquarian books on hermetic philosophy and other related subjects, has completely outgrown mine. However, this doesn't hurt our relationship. He doesn't get upset because I don't always share his enthusiasm about a new book he has acquired. He never thinks less of me because my knowledge on this subject is much less than his. I never chide him about his fascination with books, nor do I complain about the time he spends on his interest. In fact, I find the experience he gains from his love of books fascinating. I get the privilege of learning from his knowledge on the subject. It only makes him a more interesting person.

I sometimes suggest we might get more frugal in our acquisitions, but again I say, we should. I don't put the entire weight of a problem on what he's doing. It's not his responsibility alone. It's our responsibility. If we're spending too much money, we both need to cut back. We listen to each other and we have a good checks and balance system. All governments and relationships should have one. Leigh realizes that when I have a complaint about something, I deserve his attention to consider it. He may not agree with me and might present another viewpoint. I realize I may not be entirely correct in my assessment of a situation after listening to him. Hence goes mutual respect and compromise in a relationship.

Leigh has grown into a master painter during the time I have known him. I have yet to pick up a paintbrush. This disparity of growth between us is not a problem. Leigh's pursuit and love of painting has only enhanced our relationship. His growth in this area has excited me and made me proud of him. I love his work so it is easy for me to appreciate his development and ability. I'm involved in his painting just by appreciating it. My comments offer both encouragement and insight for him. Leigh isn't concerned that I don't know as much as he does about color and composition. However, I have increased my knowledge immeasurably about different artists and art styles. We can discuss art together and I can applaud his efforts, not just as a cheerleader, but as a knowledgeable partner. We have grown together even though our growth has been different or apart.

Our growth, in these cases, complements the other's. Even if I became interested in bird watching and Leigh studied archeology, it would add to our relationship. When we grow and expand, we become more interesting to each other. We have taken a journey, explored a new territory and have new ideas and stories to share. The important thing is to take the journey. When you continue to broaden your abilities and extend your intellectual reach, you become increasingly desirable. Romantic love depends on personal interest and continues with persisting curiosity. When you expand and live an ever-enlarging life, you will always be romantically intriguing. Your love for each other will only be enhanced.

Growing at Different Rates

If you and your partner have a very slow rate of growth and it works for both of you, fine. A relationship can work well if your partner has a faster rate of growth than you do as well. You can still be an interesting partner if you take the time and opportunity to grow, no matter the pace. It can also work well if the roles are reversed and you are in the fast lane of growth. All these scenarios can make a good relationship. The problem arises when you are completely dissatisfied with your partner's rate of growth, be it fast, slow or not at all. While we can always extend our intellectual reach and our interests, we can't make our partner choose to grow. If he stops being interesting or interested, you may lose interest very quickly and there isn't much you can do. It still takes two to dance life's most radiant tango. That is the heart and sometimes the disappointing crux of the matter. We can't control another person, nor should we try. We can only include and encourage our partners.

Growing With Similar Goals

It is obviously beneficial to have similar goals with the person you love. It is to be hoped that is one of the reasons you decided to share your lives together. If your goal is to have a secure lifestyle with a good job and a respected position in your community and your husband wants to see the world on a tramp steamer working at different jobs along the way, you have a problem. Your growth in accomplishing your goals may be fascinating, but will certainly not fit with his. If you're elected to the city council for four years and have a job that doesn't allow you to travel, he may be proud of you and romantically intrigued, but it hinders his plans to be a vagabond. Compromises can be made, but it would be easier and more productive if you were growing and working toward a common cause or at least not one counterproductive to the other.

What if you began your relationship with similar goals and desires and somehow one of you got left in the dust? Somehow your partner started developing in a completely different manner. Perhaps your husband discovered Buddhism when you both had been strong Catholics when you met. If my husband began investigating Buddhism I would find it interesting because I enjoy learning about new things. Even if I didn't share his fascination, I would make sure we maintained our open line of communication so we would be aware of each other's feelings along the way. I wouldn't be left in the dust. We are taking this life ride together. If he found his spiritual gratification through Buddhism, great. It would only make him a happier person. Because I respect him and his choices I would know there must be something worthwhile in Buddhism to have him convert. If the idea of my partner being a Buddhist were completely abhorrent to me after going through the discovery process with him from the beginning and discussing our thoughts along the way, I would join a convent. Just kidding. The only thing you can do is make a compromise because you love each other. If he took up an interest in robbing liquor stores that is another story. Then I would have him join a convent.

Compromise Can Be Good

Compromise has a bad reputation. Everyone thinks of it as copping out, not going for the gold, selling out. Have I used enough clichés to make my point? In my experience, compromise is a good thing. By meeting someone halfway we must at least move away from where we have been, away from any box we have created for ourselves, and explore a new area. We may have been stuck in our own minds and now we get to have a new vantage point, to see something differently, to deal with someone else's point of view.

I often say you haven't experienced parenting to its fullest if you have only one child. You never have to deal with, "Mom, Brighton is touching me with her feet. Mom, she is still doing it, make her stop" or "Why does Caytlyn get to sit in the front seat all the time? It's my turn to sit in the front seat" or "I can't believe Brighton wore my best sweater to her dance class! It's completely ruined." My normal response to these complaints is to have the girls try to solve their own problems with each other. Siblings, at least in this household, must learn the art of compromise. "You can't always get what you want," Maxim #37, courtesy of Grandma, Mick Jagger and Keith Richards.

Anyone who lives with someone else must make compromises. My roommates and I were constantly making compromises. It's the natural order of co-existing. I don't remember feeling resentful toward my roommates. It's called sharing, giving, living in peace. We could all take our toys and go play by ourselves, but somewhere along the line we found out it's much more fun to play with other people. Caytlyn may resent Brighton now and then and think how much more she would have if Brighton were not here, but when the final tally is taken, she admits she knows how much more she has because Brighton is here.

Compromise is a good thing. By cutting back on our own desires and allowing someone else to influence us, we end up broadening our horizons. It's similar to exercise. We don't always want to do it, but we feel so much better when we do. Think of it as giving ourselves a good pruning. Just like a rose or a fruit tree, we grow so much better after cutting a little away. Compromise is a tool we must learn to use to have any kind of a relationship. Give a little, take a little: "That's the glory of, that's the story of love."

Romance Can Last Forever

Just like fine wine, a relationship can mature and grow in a rich, robust manner. I hear many people say that after a few years all the thrill and excitement leaves a marriage. This is often the reason given for choosing a practical mate, a friend, not someone you are attracted to or for whom you feel romantic love. So many people attest to the fact that romance doesn't last that it must be true. They site the lack of interest many people have in their mates after even a few months together as evidence of this fact. I disagree completely. I guarantee romance can last forever in a relationship. It can even grow stronger.

When I was first with Leigh, I would tell my oldest sister how much I loved him, what a fabulous person he was, how my stomach would practically leap into my chest when he touched me. She would laugh politely and reply, "That's so sweet, but enjoy it now, because it doesn't last." After a few years when we were still in love and the romance was in full swing, she would insist that we were just newlyweds, so of course everything was joyous. "Wait until reality hits you," she would say. Future comments included, "Wait until you have children" or "Wait until you've been married as long as I have." I've reached each of my sister's benchmarks for our relationship and I've discovered she and many other people who made similar comments are wrong. You can keep the romance in your relationship. It can even grow more romantic.

When you have been with someone for years, you each know what the other enjoys in all areas of life and you are able to enhance your pleasures. You also discover new ways to be romantic. If you are creative, there are many avenues to express your love. Sometimes the old ways cannot be topped. Once your heart has beaten faster because your lover touches you, it can always beat faster. It doesn't slow down just because you have shared time together. It grows richer, fuller, just like that bottle of rare aged wine I mentioned before. For all young couples that fear romance might leave your lives as the years pass, I guarantee it can stay as long as you want it to stay and may even grow past your highest expectations. That's why they charge so much for vintage bottles of wine.

Shadow Dancing

Many times as a relationship grows couples become proficient at what is called Shadow Dancing. There are many versions of Shadow Dancing. Carl Gustav Jung, the Swiss psychologist, was one of the first to discuss and define the Shadow. The Shadow is the part of ourselves that we do not own. When this occurs, the Shadow manifests outside of us and we ultimately must deal with it. In relationships we tend to play out the Shadow projection of our partner and project our Shadow onto them. It's a two-way street. We decide who we are and what we reject or repress, consciously or unconsciously, is our Shadow and it can be played out by our partner. Maybe they give life to our darker side. Perhaps they get all our freedom. It's similar to yin/yang or masculine/feminine. The theory is that if you allow parts of yourself to go unconscious and do not express them in a healthy manner, they will inevitably manifest in your partner's behavior. Each of us lives out what our partner doesn't know or accept about himself. Our partner may be living out our best qualities. Until we get to know and come to terms with the Shadow side of ourselves, it's very difficult to put our Shadows back into our own lives.

Just after our eldest daughter, Caytlyn, was born I started feeling as if Leigh was having all the fun. Even Caytlyn seemed to have more fun than I had. I felt as if I was the responsible, mature person in the relationship. I grew much too serious, something that's not unusual after becoming a first-time mother with many new responsibilities. I was getting used to a new role for myself and consciously was only seeing a loss of my freedom, of all my fun. Unconsciously I was trying to make the new adjustments to deal with a huge change in my life. Didn't being a mother mean you had to be responsible? This was no laughing matter. Leigh seemed positively giddy by comparison. He played out my Shadow projection completely. Finally, I decided to take my Shadow back. When I reclaimed my Shadow I could finally laugh at my silly husband with our little girl. Now we could both be free, full of mirth and good parents to boot. I realized I could travel, work or play, do just about anything I wanted to do by making some adjustments instead of feeling enslaved to my situation. I didn't have to be so serious. I didn't have to lose any freedom.

About this time Leigh was offered a television show that filmed in Hong Kong. If I had remained in my oh-so-serious motherhood role, I would have begrudgingly told Leigh he could go, but I would have stayed at home with Caytlyn and felt deprived and resentful. Instead, we took Caytlyn to Hong Kong. It was a fantastic experience for all of us. At home, I would take her anywhere I wanted to go including the movies (babies sleep a lot) and roller-skating along the beach (try a baby carrier). Babies can be portable. You just have a few more accoutrements, sometimes quite a few more. It was worth it. I reclaimed my freedom so Leigh and I could find new, healthier ways to Shadow Dance.

For Leigh and me, Shadow Dancing works well. We rarely are both in a bad mood at the same time so one of us can cheer up the other one or at least not make him feel worse. There are a few practical problems that might not come from Shadow Dancing, but I lump many experiences here. Inevitably, when I am cold, Leigh is hot. This is the usual scenario, isn't it? Guys are usually hot, while we girls are freezing. "Please don't turn on the air conditioner and roll down the windows." I don't think this is an unusual request in the middle of January, but Leigh looks at me in amazement. "It's stifling in here." Now the odd thing is, when I'm hot, he's cold, so I know something strange is occurring.

Most couples can deal with temperature dilemmas. Problems seem to arise when Shadow Dancing gets more serious. When I felt resentful that Leigh was having all the fun, problems in our relationship could have developed. Resentment is similar to jealousy. It can fester and run rampant if it's not checked immediately. "Why do I have to do all the work in this relationship? I'm the only one who puts forth any effort," can grow into despising your mate and only seeing his contrary qualities. He has nowhere to go to stop the onslaught of negativity you feel for him. He can't change until you change and reclaim your Shadow.

When we start to see ourselves as victims or martyrs or anything that does not suggest equal responsibility from both partners, we can experience resentment. When this happens, stop whatever you're doing and take a good look at yourself. Are you perpetuating this feeling by not dealing with what is yours, be it your freedom, your child-like nature or your creativity? Whatever you may have repressed in yourself is screaming for expression. You must work with your Shadow to reclaim it from your partner. When you change, when you start painting or laughing or playing basketball—when you let your Shadow breathe, you will no longer feel like that victim or martyr. You will not resent your partner. Your Shadow will grow, you will grow, your relationship will grow.

~ A relationship must grow to survive. Make the necessary adjustments. You can do it.

~ Experience each phase of your relationship to its fullest. Let it evolve.

~ You cannot skip any steps.

~ Don't get out of step.

~ You don't have to grow the same way, but you must share and appreciate each other's growth. Be partners in growth.

~ Don't forget to incorporate the checks and balance system.

~ Keep lines of communication open.

~ Don't get left in the dust. Take the ride together.

~ You can only control your own growth and make yourself more romantically intriguing. You can encourage and include your partner. Never belittle him.

~ It's easier if you both have similar goals.

~ Compromise can be good. You can enjoy a new perspective.

~ Romance doesn't have to die. Keep it alive.

~ Learn how to Shadow Dance in a healthy way.

~ Stop resenting your partner by reclaiming the best parts of yourself.

~ Grow together and apart for a better life together.

Chapter Nine

KEEPING SECRETS—EACH OTHER'S

There are times when I can be a spoiler. I don't mean to undermine anyone's fun, but it's difficult to keep a secret from me. I have good intuition and know how to follow it. I also have a good sense for finding clues and reading people's faces. Sherlock Holmes would be impressed. I am one of those people who seem to know the ending of a film before the opening credits have finished. "The man in the red coat did it," I announce. "Don't tell me" is the customary response. I reply innocently that I don't know for sure, but they know and I know that I'm probably right. I end up going to movies alone quite a bit or I try to keep my mouth shut, not always successfully.

My husband has Saturn in Scorpio. Astrologically speaking this means he likes to have secrets. Non-astrologically speaking, Leigh likes to have secrets. They don't even have to be about anything very secretive. "Oh great honey," I'd say, "you had your hair cut."

"Sh! Don't tell anyone."

Leigh is a great confidant because he respects everyone's privacy and never gossips and most of all, he usually forgets what you told him.

Our eldest daughter also has Saturn in Scorpio, so I am doubly blessed. Getting information from Caytlyn is impossible, unless you approach her after nine o'clock at night. Somehow her communication skills become more active at this hour. Not much, but every little bit helps.

When you're someone who loves to have secrets, it can be difficult to have a wife and mother like me. Both Leigh and Caytlyn love to talk. They would just elect not to talk about anything too personal. Leigh prefers the world of ideas and Caytlyn—well, just wait until after 9:00 PM. They both are confirmed believers, much to their chagrin, that I know all. Leigh is comfortable with this because he knows I am non-judgmental where he is concerned, so he never gets busted by me. Caytlyn is not as sure. Even after all these years she can still be a bit nervous about Mom knowing all. Thank goodness her secrets are generally harmless and I hope she knows I would never use them against her or embarrass her with them. I often tell her this, but I don't know if she hears me. When she was younger she was amazed when I casually mentioned some incident that had previously occurred at school that I couldn't have known about. I just threw a few zingers like that in every now and then just to remind her that mother could be Big Brother if she wanted to. However, Caytlyn knows that I trust her and that I don't feel it necessary to play that role.

My ability has only enhanced my relationship with Leigh. It's one thing if you're constantly off-balance because your mate knows everything about you and might expose you at any moment; it's quite another when she knows everything about you, accepts everything about you, treasures everything about you and would never expose anything about you even in the worst of moments. Your true grit is disclosed in those awful moments when you want to hurt your partner during a heated argument. You could be capable of the most despicable behavior toward him because he may have hurt you in the most despicable manner and yet you would never think of betraying him. Leigh has no deep dark secrets, but the fact that I respect even the smallest of his secrets shows him my true grit, my true love.

Sacred Trust

Too often people use their spouse's secrets as emotional blackmail. They know their partner's weak spots and do not hesitate to pull out all the stops when it's advantageous. Your relationship is doomed the moment this happens. You have lost one of the most important elements of any marriage—trust. Your mate can no longer feel vulnerable and open with you. He will no longer have the security necessary to share his intimate self with you. Emotional roadblocks and barriers will be erected and you may spend the rest of your lives taking detours, never driving the main road together.

We live in a time of telling all. There are rarely any taboos on any subject. Watch daytime talk shows, reality TV or listen to the news. Everything you could possibly imagine and many things that would never occur to you are being discussed. We learn more about the sex life of politicians than we ever should know and all the intimate details about every celebrity than we would ever want to know. You should no longer feel alone or strange if you get excited walking in kitty litter with hot pink stiletto heels while wearing your mother's panties on your head, eating artichokes and reading Dante's Inferno. Someone was probably on television last week discussing the same thing. At the very least there was a video on YouTube all about it. While these revelations may help some people feel less alone or strange, we still struggle to relate to one another. Most of us still feel that no one could ever accept us if they knew all our secrets. Heaven forbid we tell someone! They would probably end up live and in color, discussing our secrets on prime time or Facebook.

Establishing trust in a relationship takes time. Crashing and burning trust for a lifetime can take only a second. No matter how hurt or angry you are, remember how important it is to keep each other's secrets, protect each other's confidences. Your sex life should not be the topic of conversation at the Women's Club luncheon, the annual golf tournament or even an intimate conversation with a best friend. Your wife or husband should be your best friend. Your intimate life together should be just that. You both lose when that intimacy is gone. Make a safe environment for each other. Know that you can express every part of yourself, share anything with your loved one and there will be no retributions. Know that you have a sacred trust. If you do this, you will have a bond that will sustain you through anything.

However, if you have a problem in any area of your life, be it sex or any taboo subject you may feel you have created, you should talk about it. You must first discuss any problems you have with each other and if the two of you can't resolve them, then you should consider getting outside advice.

Honesty Is Not Always The Best Policy

I'm not saying that you must always be completely honest with your mate. There are times when Grandma's Maxim #6, "Honesty is the best policy," is not appropriate. If there is a choice in the reply to a question such as "How do I look?" and you hate what your spouse is wearing, I would suggest, "I think your blue dress looks better on you" as opposed to "You look fat in that outfit." Too often we excuse blatant cruelty by saying, "I was just being honest." In the movement towards voicing our true feelings and not holding back, we can confuse honesty with a lack of tact. We forget basic kindness and manners. There are many ways to say the same thing. If it's a question of hurting someone you love, choose the softer, gentler way.

We must also examine our motives: are we trying to help our mate by being honest, or do we want to get a little barb in there and inflict some pain because of perceived slights we have previously felt from our mates?

A dear friend of ours, Franklyn, announced one day that henceforth he was going to be completely honest. He was sick of pretending to like something when he did not, of doing things he really didn't want to do. We can all relate to his revelation. I was surprised by Franklyn's sudden enlightenment, however, because I had always found him to be quite forthright and occasionally a bit caustic in his remarks before he avowed his conversion to complete honesty. I realized I better fasten my seatbelt for a bumpy ride whenever I was with him.

One evening we invited Franklyn to accompany us to a party. We arrived at a sedate gathering with a few people chatting, but nothing too exciting or interesting happening. We've all been in similar situations. When they occur, you stay for a time and then say your farewells to the host. That's usually what happens, but this particular night Franklyn took it upon himself to announce how boring the party was and how he would not waste his time with dull people discussing tedious topics. With that, he promptly left.

To Franklyn, he was being honest about his feelings; to everyone else he was being mean and rude. It was not necessary for him to belittle everyone. No one had asked nor cared about his opinion. He could have bid farewell and thanked the host for inviting him. He would not have compromised any of his desires; he would have left and could have declined all future invitations. Obviously he had never heard Grandma's Maxim #76, "If you can't say anything nice, don't say anything at all."

Franklyn's poor behavior seems obvious, but many of us have probably adopted a similar stance at some time, hopefully to a lesser degree. If you have mean-spirited feelings about someone or something, I suggest you keep them a secret and find another way of expressing yourself less harmfully.

I tend to be frank with friends and family when they request my opinion. I don't think you should sidestep a question when someone may need to hear the truth. You might be the only person who can tell him the truth. If you have developed sacred trust with your partner, you know you can tell him what he must hear in the most loving way possible and he will know that it is without judgement. If he is drinking too much, for example, you must address the problem directly. Be especially honest about things he can fix. However, if he made a faux pas while speaking to the president of his company, no need to say, "Boy, were you stupid." I'm sure he realizes that. Approach each situation as the situation dictates. Examine your motives. You don't have to keep all your feelings a secret, just express them in a compassionate manner.

Giving Secrets Light

Do you remember how horrible you felt as a child when your best friend told your special secret to the entire student body? You probably felt humiliated and most of all betrayed and alone. You knew you could no longer share your complete self with anyone. No one could know how you felt, what you dreamed. Those secrets would remain guarded, hidden away. Some of those secrets would shrivel and die deep within you, never exposing them again. The fear of feeling humiliated or inferior or even different was too overwhelming.

When Leigh and I were first together he kept his drawings in a big black portfolio and his poetry in various journals concealed from an intruder's eye. He never shared his creations with anyone. When I finally saw his drawings and read his poetry, I was amazed. His work was awe-inspiring. Leigh was surprised by my reaction. He thought no one could appreciate his work. He was not insecure about his creations nor doubtful of his ability. He knew his work was great and it wasn't out of a feeling of vulnerability that he kept it secreted away. It was a feeling of extreme pride that kept it hidden from public consumption. He doubted anyone could understand his work and value it as he did.

I opened a door for Leigh quite by chance. In this case, I did not keep a secret. I gave the secret light. A person's dreams, ambitions and creations may be hidden away for years. In a good relationship, a person must know his partner will accept and encourage all his secret dreams. In an atmosphere of love and support your partner will feel safe and know you will encourage him in his pursuits because they are important to him.

~ Develop sacred trust so you can be all that you are with your partner.

~ Give each other the environment where you can share your secrets, where your confidences are protected, where hidden dreams can flourish.

~ Know that your intimacies will be private between the two of you.

~ Never use your partner's secrets as emotional or any other kind of blackmail.

~ Gaining trust takes time, but losing it can only take a moment.

~ Accept each other's secrets and treasure them. Show true grit by never betraying them. Your love will flourish and grow.

Chapter Ten

SENSATIONAL SEX

I met Leigh the first day in my filmmaking career. I found him handsome, intriguing, pleasant, full of energy and a bit strange in a wonderful way. Leigh says that from the moment he met me, every time he was near me his heart started to beat faster. We both remember early morning calls and a very tiny hall that led to the make-up room. We would pass each other, Leigh with a bag and a guitar in hand which made the already small space even smaller. We inevitably brushed against each other for a few seconds in the dark. My stomach would flip-flop whenever this happened. Leigh with a pounding heart and I with a nauseous stomach. What a great pair. That was more than thirty years ago and Leigh still insists I make his heart beat faster and I feel the same excitement.

Inexplicable Chemistry

People share a natural chemistry. On an atomic level we're made of energy, so it makes sense that we have an attraction to other masses of energy. I have experienced this attraction, be it slight or great. I have also experienced aversion and a desire to get away from some people, not because I feared them, but because I felt a negative, repellent force from them. Other times I feel nothing from people. They are just there and I'm not drawn to interact with them. They may have wonderful chemistry with someone else, but for me—nada. When we are lucky enough to feel that wonderful interactive net drawing us together with someone else, all of our molecules seem to sing and rejoice. We calm each other's soul, ignite each other's passions.

During my eldest sister, Lynne's, dating period after her divorce, my mother would often suggest someone she thought was fun and interesting for Lynne to consider. My mother couldn't understand when Lynne would stop seeing an eligible bachelor because, as Lynne said, "There's no chemistry between us." I can sympathize with both points of view. My mother didn't comprehend why Lynne didn't want to be with a nice person and go out with him. Chemistry might come later, and if it didn't, so be it. At least she wouldn't be alone. In past generations women didn't often consider chemistry. They married the finest, most dependable man and made the best of it for a lifetime. Lynne, on the other hand, could never be with someone for whom she had no attraction. This had been her way, with good and bad results, but she was willing to accept those results or be alone. She understood Grandma's Maxim #77, "The biggest temptation is to settle for too little." Lynne knew what she wanted and would not settle for less.

When Leigh was going to Juilliard he dated a variety of girls, but felt empty and alone even when he was with them. He finally realized that he wanted, like the poet Rainer Maria Rilke writes, "To be with those who know secret things or else alone." Leigh still feels the same. It's not a melancholy feeling, but one of self-worth. He knows he has much to accomplish and doesn't want to waste his valuable time to just be with someone.

We all makes choices. It's up to the individual to decide what is important in a relationship. Chemistry isn't something one chooses. Leigh and I were lucky that we experienced and still experience chemistry along with the other qualities necessary for a good relationship. There are others who have felt chemistry with someone and ended up having a disastrous relationship. The chemistry either burned itself out or those involved forgot about a few other ingredients that are necessary to sustain the chemistry, such as love and commitment. Chemistry is great, however, and can lead to amazing intimate, sensual experiences shared with your cherished and adored lab partner. The Bunsen burner's flame is bright as the molecules begin to bond. I know Mr. McCully, my high school chemistry teacher, would be proud to know that I have taken his lessons to such a level.

Feelings—Nothing More Than Feelings

Both men and women find it difficult to separate how they feel and how sexually attracted they are to a person. We know how difficult it is to jump in bed with someone who has been criticizing us all day. It's difficult to detach our heads from our bodies. No one is going to feel romantic about someone he's been bickering with for the last two days. Maybe that was what Grandma was hinting at when she said, "Never go to bed angry," Maxim #13. I agree with Grandma one hundred per cent, but in this case maybe Grandma meant to say, never go to bed with someone with whom you are angry. If you do, don't expect terrific sex.

I first realized how powerful one's feelings are when I was in college. I'd been dating a young man for some time and knew he was serious about me. I had always cared for him a great deal. I enjoyed kissing him and certainly had that tingly feeling whenever I was with him. It was nothing like the tidal wave that was to hit me when I met Leigh, but definitely a positive attraction. One evening he told me that he had been seeing other women, a lot of other women, and sleeping with quite a few. He never had much of a relationship with any of them;

most were one-night stands. He was away from me most of the week while I was at school, so he found himself with free time on his hands. I knew he was being honest when he told me he only loved me, wanted to marry me and that these other women meant nothing to him.

Once I found out about his affairs, something happened to me that I couldn't control. My feelings completely changed. Grandma had told me, "Good to forgive, best to forget," Maxim #12, but when he touched my hand, I felt repulsed. Any feeling for him vanished. I understand many women might have this reaction, but it seemed strange to me. Someone I had once enjoyed holding and kissing I no longer wanted to be near. This was not a temporary feeling. I never wanted to be touched by this man again. It was not an intellectual decision, it was strictly involuntary. I wasn't devastated by the news of my boyfriend's unfaithfulness, yet I could no longer tolerate his touch. I was fascinated by my reaction in an almost scientific way. How could I have changed so quickly? Obviously, I wasn't really in love with him, but my reaction proved to me how much feelings have to do with physical desire.

Having a great sexual relationship with someone depends on how you feel about him, not just your sexual prowess together. You can go through all the right moves, but if you have unresolved negative feelings for your partner the earth is not going to move and the bells will not ring. You must deal with those issues if you want to have great sex. If you feel your wife is frigid, use a little self-examination. How do you treat her when you're not in the bedroom? It's not easy to switch channels after hearing negative comments all day. Be loving outside the bedroom to have any chance of really being loved in the bedroom.

Do Not Save Sexy for the Bedroom

Everyone has heard about how exciting it can be to have sex in the woods, the airplane lavatory, the corner telephone booth or on the trampoline in the backyard. Although some of these sites don't excite me, if that's what inspires you, go for it. As Grandma would say, "Live and let live," Maxim #5. I'm talking about being and feeling sexy anytime, anywhere. I'm not advocating public groping around the clock. I'm suggesting much subtler, but provocative behavior of which only you and your mate will be aware.

It's important to feel and be sexy with each other any time you are together. Maybe not every time, just any time. Don't save those little innuendoes, touches and looks for the bedroom. Know the great feeling when you are desired by and desirous of your mate many different times during the day. It can be as subtle as running your hand down his leg or back with that sly come hither stare Sinatra sings about while your lover is putting away the laundry or perhaps a few words whispered intimately while sitting next to each other in a movie theatre. Maybe it is you wearing that red dress he loves at dinner one night. Your children may wonder why you're dressed up to stay home, but in our family the unusual is the norm, so they don't think about it too much.

Leigh makes me feel sexy. He can put his arms around me and say, " You feel so good," in a way that makes me melt. When this happens, it is kind of the chicken and the egg syndrome. I find myself being sexy. It doesn't matter which came first; it's just a good syndrome to have. Don't be afraid to experience each other's sensuality and be sensual any time. You don't have to jump each other's bones on the kitchen floor. It is just an affirmation of I am woman, you are man, and ain't that grand.

For Play

In every aspect of a relationship playfulness is important, but perhaps most important in sex. How could we forget how much fun it is to play? We certainly knew it as children, but somehow the bell rang, recess was over and a voice said, "You're an adult now, no more playing." What a silly voice and so many of us think we hear it.

My sister came home from college one weekend at the ripe old age of twenty-one dragging a huge suitcase behind her. She announced to me that she was giving me all her clothes because they were much too young for her now and she had to start dressing like an adult. My sister was always conservative so I assure you these clothes were not tie-dyed T-shirts, wild bell-bottoms or fringed suede jackets. I took my new bonanza gladly, but her behavior baffled me. She was one of those people who heard the voice and believed she had to become an adult and that being an adult meant doing nothing outlandish–no silly, adolescent behavior allowed.

That voice never spoke to me. I still wear unusual clothes, have water fights, do cartwheels and wrestle on the front lawn. No one seems to notice. The usual reason people give for surrendering this type of behavior is, "What would people say!" They don't realize most people don't notice someone else's behavior because they're caught up in their own world and probably acting stranger than you are. Even Grandma knew the value of play, "The family that plays together, stays together," Grandma's Maxim #22. I know this is true. Laughing and galloping through the fields can help any relationship with your children or your spouse. Wrestling on the grass or in bed can lead to all sorts of wonderful things. You start laughing and feeling great all over. "Laughter is the best medicine," Grandma's Maxim #15. Many studies have proven this theory, but when you're laughing with the person you love, you know it's true.

Laughter can be wonderful foreplay. You feel happy and close to the one you love. Never be such an adult that you forget how to play, how to be joyful. It's the secret ingredient for great sex and a great life.

Never Be Too Busy for Sex

Rush rush here, rush rush there. Get the children to school, go to work, do errands, clean the house. It's amazing there is time for anything except the bare necessities. Make sex one of the bare necessities. Schedule an appointment if need be, but don't be too busy to be intimate with your partner.

When I was working on a particularly difficult show, Leigh was protective of me. He made sure I rested as much as possible and took care of everything he could take care of to save me from doing it. One evening he kept trying to get me to go to bed to get some much-needed sleep. I looked at him forlornly and said how much I missed being with him. He wanted to be with me, but knew I needed to rest. He didn't think I'd want to make love with him with everything else that was going on. "No," I replied, "I need to be with you even more when things are so crazy. It doesn't matter if I'm exhausted. I'm more renewed, just by being with you." It was a relief for both of us to realize this. Too often couples go for long periods of time under the misguided idea that they are too busy to be intimate with each other. When they finally make time for one another they realize what they've been missing, how wonderful it feels to be together, and that they should do it more often.

Sometimes couples must be very protective of their time together.

Turn off the telephone and computer, come home early from work, visit your mate at work — just make sure you have time to be together. I know couples that have certain nights they either go out on a date or make sure they are undisturbed at home. They know the value of time spent together. You can both get so involved in everything you're doing individually that you lose any sense of having another person be a part of your life. You're living the two ships passing in the night syndrome. Don't let it happen. Come into the harbor right now and take a cruise together. Always remember to remember how great it feels to hold and touch one another. Do not forget again!

Use It or Lose It

Grandma was referring to one's brain when she would say, "Use it or lose it," Maxim #31, but I think it's an important philosophy for any part of our body. It's important to look and feel as good as you can for yourself and for your mate.

How many women would go to work in ripped and stained flannel nightgowns with curlers in their hair and not even a trace of lipstick? How many men would go to the market unshaven and sweaty in soiled sweatpants and a t-shirt? How many of you look like this or worse every night you are home with your husband or wife? You dress up for people you don't care about and look your worst for the person you love the most. It is important to feel relaxed in your own home. It is the one place where you don't have to create any facades. However, you can feel comfortable and still care enough to comb your hair and wear something attractive around the house. You don't have to go around fully made-up, but taking a little time to look as nice as you can will make you feel better about yourself and surprise your mate who thought you gave up caring about how you looked right after you said, "I do."

"You can't tell a book by its cover," Grandma's Maxim #20, but we should take more pride in our covers and care more about looking our best for our mates and for ourselves. Some people forget about basic exercise or even hygiene. They gain seventy-five pounds, forget to bathe regularly and can't understand why their mate doesn't seem to be as sexually attracted to them as they once were. You can only make love in the dark or change in the bathroom for so long before it's time to take action. You can make bathing a sensuous experience in itself, alone or with your partner. There's nothing like warm water, candles, bath oils and all those wonderful aromas and sensations. It can set the mood and accomplish cleanliness and godliness. You'll feel more desirable and much healthier if you maintain your weight and body tone with exercise and a healthy diet. Your partner will be proud that you care enough to try to be healthy and look as good as you can. You both will be happier and you'll start looking and feeling even more beautiful. Grandma always said, "There is no cosmetic for beauty like happiness," Maxim #9. I guess you could call it Grandma's own Love Potion #9.

The difficult part is being disciplined enough to do it. My friend is a beautiful young woman. She was always thin, but in the last few years she has put on too much weight. I try to give her a few suggestions.

"Take a walk or run every day," I say.

"I work long hours and I am too tired," is the reply.

"Try dancing or kick boxing."

"I don't have enough time or money for classes."

I suggest she listen to Oprah Winfrey's tape, which has some good ideas for getting in shape.

"If I had a staff of people pushing me to lose weight and making me exercise, I could do it too," is her response.

Wait a minute. Even if Oprah can afford help, she was still the one who had to get out there and do it. Besides, learn from what she did; utilize the experience for which she spent so much money. You can use it for free.

There are plenty of people who do it on their own. They don't always like to take their daily walk, but they do it. They just do it. When it comes right down to it, you have to decide to do it and you have to do it. I know my friend will have to decide to do it on her own. When people offer an excuse for every suggestion you offer them, it is a big clue that they're not ready to make any changes. All you can do is give them your best thoughts and silently hope those ideas might take root and one day blossom.

Frequent Frederick's or Victoria's

I have only purchased a few items at Victoria's Secret and I have never bought anything at the sexy lingerie store, Frederick's of Hollywood, but wherever you choose to shop, be sure to buy silky, lacy, satiny, lovely lingerie. You'll feel more sensual and I know your mate will appreciate your attire. This can apply to men and women. They have silk boxers and lounging pajamas for men that I know feel great to touch and must be comfortable to wear. The old utilitarian underwear that is stretched out or held together with a safety pin has to go. This alone can make a huge difference in your love life.

One day my girlfriend, Claire, asked me about buying lingerie. She confided in me that she never thought much about underwear. She just wore the standard military issues from 1994, but her husband suggested she might want to get some nicer things. He had bought her a pretty nightgown which she thought was lovely, but she wasn't sure if she should save it for when they made love or actually wear it to bed. She was accustomed to taking off all her clothes whenever she and her husband decided to make love and going from there, strictly in the buff.

I encouraged Claire to buy some nice lingerie and to wear something sensual every day. At the end of the week she reported back to me ecstatically. She had purchased some beautiful things and she felt great when she wore them. Even when no one else knew she was wearing anything special, she felt luxurious and feminine in the best way. Her husband's reaction was positive to say the least. He couldn't stop telling her how beautiful she looked. He loved going to bed with her and waking up beside her. She also discovered something with which I definitely agree. Most people look much sexier dressed in beautiful lingerie than they do dressed in their birthday suit. It's called titillating the senses and it's always fun to do.

Familiar Fantasizing

We all have fantasies. It's great when you can share those fantasies with your lover and make them come true. It's wonderful to feel free to explore with your partner and to experience each other in the most intimate ways.

Cindy, another girlfriend of mine, was married quite young. She wasn't experienced and was the type of woman who would do anything to please her man. She told me that when she and her husband, Mike, made love, he would look at pictures of other women from Playboy or whatever other magazine he had by the bed. This bothered her, but she never said anything to him about it. She wished he would look at her and wondered if there was something wrong with her.

I encouraged Cindy to tell Mike how she felt. Maybe he didn't realize how his behavior affected her. It might be as simple as that. If there were other problems, they might need counseling together, but first she should try talking to her husband. I gave the benefit of the doubt to Mike. Maybe he didn't realize what a jerk he was.

This one-sided type of fantasizing is not good for a relationship and can be demeaning to your lover. If you fantasize about someone, try fantasizing about your mate. Yes, that same person who's lying next to you in bed, the one who brushes his teeth next to you, the one you love and adore. Who else would you want to fantasize about anyway? Some silly movie star you don't know and probably wouldn't like if you got to know?

Unfortunately, Cindy and Mike had many other problems besides his extracurricular fantasizing in bed and ended up divorced. When you see an erotic scene in a movie or read something sensual in a novel, if you focus on that scenario and exclude your mate, it takes the attention away from your partner and your relationship. The same scene or passage could greatly enhance the relationship you have with your lover, but you must make him a part of the experience. Try it, you'll both like it.

The Great Art of Massage

When I come home from work, my mind is in a thousand places, thinking about everything I must do, am doing or have done. It takes some time for me to get back in my body and experience the now. Leigh can tell when it's been one of those days. The last thing I'm thinking about is Leigh and me touching and being close to one another. I have too much to do even if it's what I should be thinking about the most. Like people living in the city who must go to the country and hug a tree to feel grounded, I need to hug a Leigh.

Leigh starts by giving me a light massage. I can feel my body tense in the very beginning. It's as if I can't allow myself to relax and experience pleasure. So much to do. Leigh continues undaunted. It's interesting how I metamorphose. The caterpillar turns into the butterfly as my senses are activated once again. Never underestimate the value of massage and learn how to touch each other in the best way. It's not only very healthy, it feels really good. For anyone who isn't in the mood, try a little massage. Voila! It can be a great aphrodisiac.

Sacred Sex

The sexual experience can be cosmic, transforming and transcendental. There is nothing more intimate than a spiritual connection demonstrated sensually. It becomes spiritual ecstasy, a union of consciousness and energy. The erotic experience is timeless, an experience of transcendence beyond normal worldly limitations, a penetration into the depths of space. You are pulled out into the universe, beyond all-knowable things or events. It is an experience of creative energy, the power of transformation, an uplifting and liberating force that leads to the ecstasy of fulfillment, the union of the male and female in each of you. And you say you would rather watch TV?

There is a wide range of sexual experiences, but know that the experience described above is definitely possible. You won't find this experience listed under position #53 in the latest "You Too Can Have Great Sex" book, although it's always fun to experiment. But after you've read all the books, seen all the films and tried all the various aids to ecstasy, try being with the person you love more than anything in the world. Look into his eyes, hold him, touch him, caress him. You'll become overwhelmed by your feelings, the sensations of each other's body and you'll begin your journey. Let me know when you get back to earth. Maybe that was what Ralph Cramden meant when he said, "To the moon, Alice!"

Sexual Misconceptions

No, this isn't about the real location of the G spot or the truth about clitoral vs. vaginal orgasms. This is about realizing that men and women are individuals. They each have their own likes and dislikes, faults and virtues. There is no all men prefer this or all women hate that. For every man you find who likes one thing, you'll find another who hates it. Don't act according to other people's generalizations. Find out what your mate likes, her passions and desires, her fantasies, her sensitive areas. Know everything about her, not 72% of the population or whatever the latest demographics are in a certain poll. Who fills out those polls anyway?

I go to a wonderful ballet class, but every now and then many of the women in the class complain about how despicable men are and it drives me crazy. They say that men are all terrible, they have no idea how to appreciate a good woman, they cannot commit. Gosh, these men really sound awful. I ask the women who they're dating, what kind of men they know and where they meet these misfits? The usual response is, "It doesn't matter. They're all alike."

I disagree. The men I know aren't misfits. They're interesting, articulate, sensitive, funny — all the things we say we want in a man.

Of course if I were a man, I wouldn't find many of these complaining women attractive. They seem hard and domineering. Every man I've met in my life wasn't always wonderful. I've known some real stinkers, but they were all their very own individual type of stinker. Some were just semi-stinkers. In other words, stop classifying all men or all women under one heading. See everyone as the individual they are.

~ There's a natural chemistry between people. Experiencing this chemistry is sensational, but make sure you develop the love and commitment to sustain the attraction.

~ We can't separate our heads from our bodies. Be loving outside the bedroom to have any chance of experiencing true love in the bedroom.

~ Deal with the negative issues in your relationship if you want to have great sex.

~ Don't save sexy for the bedroom.

~ Feel and be sexy any time you're together. It will keep your relationship sensuous.

~ Celebrate your sexuality.

~ Never grow too old to play.

~ Remember the secret ingredients for great sex and a great life—laughter and joy.

~ Never be too busy for sex.

~ When you're stressed and overwhelmed with too much to do is when you need your partner most.

~ Protect your time together.

~ Remember how great it feels to hold and touch each other.

~ Use it or lose it.

~ Look and feel the best you can for yourself and your mate.

~ Eat right, exercise and do not forget Grandma's Maxim #48, "Cleanliness is next to godliness."

~ Eat, exercise and bathe together.

~ You know what you have to do to get in shape, so do it.

~ Wear beautiful lingerie. It will arouse both of you.

~ Fantasize about your mate. Include him in your erotic dreams.

~ Try massaging each other. It's a great aphrodisiac even when you're not in the mood.

~ Remember men and women are individuals with different tastes and desires. Challenge yourself to refrain from stereotyping people.

~ There are good people of both sexes. Love the good.

Chapter Eleven

CARETAKERS OF PRECIOUS SOULS

Leigh never thought he would get married until he was in his forties. Consequently he was as surprised as I was when, at the ripe old age of twenty-two, he bounded up the stairs one evening, opened my bedroom door and asked a very sleepy me to marry him.

Leigh and his best friend, Bones, had been talking about me. I had gone to bed earlier since Bones and Leigh tended to talk the night away. Leigh said he should marry me. Bones agreed. Leigh tends to act immediately on some things and this was one of them. Up the stairs he ran. I said yes and went back to sleep. Leigh went downstairs and continued talking the night away with Bones.

Sometime after we were married I started thinking about having a child. I had always loved children and knew I would have my own one day. I assumed Leigh felt the same, but had never discussed it with him. Everyone loves children, right? Not necessarily so. Leigh said he didn't want children. We were happy together and he didn't want anything to spoil our relationship. He thought he was too selfish to be a good father.

After I picked up my jaw from the floor, I realized I had to alter my plans. I didn't react hysterically to what my new husband told me. Maybe I intuitively knew that what he said was not a forever statement, even though he thought it was. In retrospect it was good that I responded to Leigh's pronouncement the way I did: I only told him that I had planned on having children and I thought he would be a wonderful father. I didn't harp on the situation and I didn't plan to go ahead and have a child anyway without my husband's consent.

As time passed, having a child didn't seem as important to me. I still believed Leigh would be a wonderful father. I could see how caring he was with our pets. Equating caring for children with caring for pets may offend some people, but I believe how a man cares for his pets can be a good clue to how he will care for his children. You can't necessarily tell if a man will be a good father by how he acts with other children. Leigh didn't have much interest in other children at the time. What I realized was that those children were not his children. His pets were his pets. His interaction with Chester, our chinchilla, showed me much more about how he would be as a parent than how he reacted to someone else's child crying on an airplane. Leigh's care and patience with Chester convinced me that he would be a good father.

Even though I wanted children and thought Leigh would be an excellent father, I was ready to forego parenthood because both parents must be committed to having a child. It's one of the most important decisions you'll make in your life and it's not fair to the unborn child to come into this world if both parents are not committed to his upbringing and welfare.

If having a child is paramount to you, make sure you settle the issue before you marry. Don't break whatever agreement you make. It's not fair to the person you are bringing into the world and will only foster resentment in your relationship with your partner. Commitments made to each other must be kept unless you both agree to amend or change them as you grow and change.

Parenthood Is Not for Wimps

After about three years of marriage, Leigh changed his mind about wanting a family. He described his decision as a light went on in his head and heart and he knew having children was the right thing for us. This complete shift was not prompted by anything I was aware of. We entered into parenthood with much joy and excitement.

Caytlyn was probably one of the most well traveled fetuses in history. Leigh was on the television show, *Dallas*, when she was conceived. In our first trimester, the cast of the show was invited to Israel and directly after that trip we toured Ireland and the British Isles. Immediately following that, during our second trimester, Leigh did a tour on the *Love Boat* throughout the Mediterranean. The rest of the cast all contributed something to our soon-to-be-born baby. Shirley Jones gave me the idea for Caytlyn's name (an unusual one at that time, but now quite common), Linda Evans did her numerology, and Debbie Allen taught her father how to dance. Everyone seemed to give us some words of wisdom. Needless to say it was an enjoyable few months of being pregnant.

In our third trimester we were off to Sicily where Leigh was filming *Hearts in Armor.* We spent our free time with two of the other actors in the film, Rick Edwards and Ronn Moss, both of whom are extremely good-looking men. Add my husband to the mix and one has quite a trio of handsome guys. I must have made an impression in those little Sicilian towns with my three escorts and my gigantic belly. I changed a few Sicilian minds about pregnant women being unattractive to men. In my condition I had three knockouts, all being attentive to my every need. Could the secret be my huge stomach? I probably increased the birth rate on the island 50% that year.

Leigh and I were prepared to have Caytlyn in Sicily, as we didn't want to be apart for this momentous occasion. My obstetrician, Paul Crane, scouted Sicilian doctors and hospitals for me on his trip to Italy. After he told me that birthing conditions in Sicily were still much like the conditions in the United States in the 1950s, i.e. forceps babies with anesthetized moms, we began to reevaluate the situation.

Our friend, Rick, offered to help Leigh deliver our baby in the hotel room as he had just aided in the birth of his first daughter and felt qualified to now become a midwife. Even though Leigh and I had attended many birthing classes and read many books on the subject, we decided to decline Rick's offer. We knew it was necessary for me to go back to the United States.

The production company was gracious enough to allow Leigh to come home for our due date, but Caytlyn had a surprise for us. She decided she wasn't going to make an appearance at that time and Leigh had to return to Italy. Days passed, weeks passed, and Caytlyn still didn't arrive. She was either waiting for her father to return or had decided to become a Sagittarius to continue her travelin' ways. Ultimately, she missed her father's return by a day, but completed the second goal of becoming a Sagittarius. Paul Crane was a good stand-in for Leigh as he went above and beyond his duty as our obstetrician and every one of our dear male friends was great as Caytlyn's new daddy. They caused quite a stir at Cedars Sinai Hospital, as only the father of the child is allowed to visit immediately after the birth. All of our male friends decided to visit and as soon as one of them left the maternity ward, a different one would show up claiming to be Caytlyn's new father. Our friends come from a variety of ethnic backgrounds so the nurses were sure I must have been a great ambassador to the United Nations.

Caytlyn's arrival after the onset of labor was almost as long as her in utero confinement or so it seemed to her completely exhausted mother. The good news is that, in the end, I didn't remember the pain: "What was hard to endure can be sweet to recall," Grandma's Maxim #24. This is true about parenthood in general. Since that first day, when you look back at all the moments with your children, the negative seems to fade. Even so, you must go into parenthood with open eyes, ready to no longer put your own needs first. Parenthood is not for selfish people. Leigh was right to decline fatherhood as long as he felt he couldn't be completely giving to a child. One should never have children because of other people's expectations. The desire must awaken with its own natural timing and grace. Leigh had originally thought he didn't want children, but now he couldn't live without them. Still it was necessary for both of us to be ready to commit to parenthood.

Parenthood is not for wimps. You must be responsible. You can't retire from this job. It's a lifelong commitment, no divorces here. Until we prepare for and accept our responsibilities as caretakers of precious souls and do not put responsibility on the schools or nannies to raise our children, we can't expect to leave a legacy of responsible, whole human beings to enrich our world.

Avoid Parenting Pitfalls That Can Harm Your Relationship

Your relationship will go through changes when you have children. They can be wonderful changes or they can harm your relationship with your mate. It all depends on the two of you. If you approach parenthood as a partnership and share the joys and work involved, your lives will be enhanced. If one partner feels he is the sole caregiver for the children, trouble is brewing. There will be resentment if one of you has the majority of responsibilities. Trade off as caregivers now and then; it's even more important to switch roles now. The person who is with the children most will undoubtedly get burned out and need a break. Your children can suffer as well. They benefit from the varied influences each of you bring to their lives.

Don't always put the needs or desires of your children ahead of your mate's. My friend, Victoria, was a master at this. It seemed as if her husband, Steven, was invisible when the children were around. Victoria didn't consciously do this. She was so involved with her girls that she was blind to the effect it was having on her relationship with her husband. At dinner, she made sure the girls had the first servings of food and that they were well attended. If her girls needed help with anything Victoria was there for them, but Steven soon became a third party in his own home. As a result, he began to distance himself more and more from Victoria and even from his girls.

I didn't want to repeat my friend's mistakes, so I made it clear to our girls that we wanted to make sure Daddy knew how special he was to all of us. It became a natural part of our behavior to show Leigh how glad we were to have him with us. Our behavior initiated the same behavior from him and we all felt special as a result. Even the children can be involved in getting the wheel going in the right direction.

When you have children there is less time for the two of you to be together. It's wonderful to be together as a family, but you still need one-on-one time with your mate. Make time to be together, even when the children are tiny and seem to constantly need you. This is essential. You can lose touch with each other and won't be able to be good parents because you won't be good partners. Now it's even more important to solve problems that may arise between the two of you or with your children and to express your love for one another. You now have others to consider. Your behavior can add to the joy of their lives or to their misery. You can only solve problems and remain intimate by taking the time to be together and to love one another.

Be affectionate with each other, even in front of your children - especially in front of your children. I know people that have never seen their parents embrace. I think it's important for your children to see how much you adore each other. Leigh and I hug and kiss in front of our girls all the time. We dance together, wrestle, play and tease. I can see the joy the girls feel when they see Leigh and me happy together. It's reassuring for children to know how much their parents love each other. Grandma was right when she said, "The best thing parents can do for their children is to love one another," Maxim #35.

Variety Is the Spice of Life

Leigh and I brought two different influences to our children and I feel they're the better for it. I'm more structured than Leigh and my family jokingly calls me the Japanese mother or Tiger Mom, although either can be an appropriate title. I expect much from our girls. I expect them to try to do their best in whatever they pursue. I sometimes wish I could be more relaxed along this line and am working on the ability to let them "smell the roses" more because I know how important that is. The girls are lucky to have Leigh as a father, especially as a balance to my personality. Leigh is calm, loving and supportive. They often smell the roses with Leigh. If he ever gets angry, the children know it's with good cause and they note what he has to say. Mom loses her temper a bit more frequently (I'm working on this as well) so my comments are not always taken as seriously.

Even though Leigh and I are very different types of parents and bring different influences to our children, we are partners in their upbringing. We present a united front when we deal with any serious situation. There is no confusion with our children because Mom said yes and Dad said no. If we disagree about a certain approach to a problem, we try to discuss it together before we talk about it with the girls. Don't try to solve your disagreements in front of your children. We have the deep bond of our great love for our girls in common which helps us work together in their best interests. Other parents who have this bond continue to bicker about any solution to a problem and criticize each other in front of their children. Even if you have every right to be upset with your mate, refrain from bashing him in front of your children. Work out any disagreements you have regarding each other or your children privately and then talk to the children.

All for One and One for All

Leigh, Caytlyn, Brighton and I are a family. We are all responsible for our family and we have instilled this idea in our children. As Grandma and the Three Musketeers once said, "All for one and one for all," Maxim #61. A family is a team. Each of our actions affects not only ourselves, but also each other. The girls have been brought up with this idea so they believe in it. It's a short hand to remind them of appropriate behavior. They realize our individual behavior affects the whole family. If we are out in public and the girls decide to get a little rambunctious, all we say is, "You represent the family, not just yourself." It doesn't always work, but it's usually quite effective because they know what is expected of them. When we ask one of them to clean up dishes that were left behind and they say, "They're not mine," they now know what our response will be. We all live in our home together. Each of us has the responsibility to keep it clean. We must help and be there for each other. This is a given and we must all act accordingly.

One day some years ago, Brighton was playing at a friend's house and Leigh, Caytlyn, and I were out by the pond having a glorious afternoon together. Caytlyn was enjoying herself, but suddenly a melancholy look appeared on her face. I asked her what was wrong and she said, "Brighton isn't here and it seems like a piece of the puzzle is missing." I was touched by her words because Caytlyn was not always so open with her feelings, especially concerning her little sister. I needed to remind her occasionally of the many times she told Leigh and me that she wanted a little sister because "it gets lonely when you're the only child." We had always planned on having another child, but it was great that Caytlyn decided she wanted to have one as well. She teases us every now and then when Brighton is being an annoying little sister, and says, "Why did I ever ask for her? You should have realized I was too young to know what I was saying." It was good to know that Caytlyn still missed that piece of the puzzle when Brighton was gone. The missing puzzle piece is a good analogy for us. Now whenever one of us is away and we miss her, we all use the phrase, "a piece of the puzzle is missing." It just feels better when we are all together. The puzzle is complete.

Listen and Understand Before You Try To Be Understood

Leigh often acts as the moderator in family discussions and I am thankful that he does. So often misunderstandings occur because we have not heard what another person is trying to say to us or understood what motivated his behavior. Leigh is excellent at helping each of us understand one another's behavior when we have a family meeting regarding a problem. Sometimes Caytlyn is upset because she wants to spend a day with her friends. I would prefer that she be with us because I have not seen much of her in the last week. It's often easier for each of us to understand each other when Leigh explains to Caytlyn what I'm feeling and vice versa.

Disagreements occur when people don't hear each other, though they may be screaming at the top of their lungs. The argument usually escalates with each person overstating her position and not hearing what the other person is saying. If you choose to listen to the other person before continuing with your comments, you may be surprised by what they're actually saying. Remember Grandma's Maxim #25, "The first duty of love is to listen." In my case with Caytlyn, she interpreted my wish for her to stay home as trying to control and limit her social life. I interpreted her desire to be with her friends as a desire not to spend any time with me. Leigh could explain both positions to each of us so we could see both points of view. We ended up in a compromise with Caytlyn spending part of her time with her friends and part with her family and we were both happy. It was not the compromise that accomplished this, it was the understanding we gleaned from knowing how each other felt and why.

It's not necessary to have a third party mediate, but it's obviously easier. The third person is a neutral observer and has nothing to gain in the conflict. Both sides recognize this and can listen more easily and accept a new point of view. Ideally we can learn to be our own mediators and listen to what our children or spouses or friends are trying to tell us and endeavor to understand them before we try to make our point and be understood. When we truly understand, we don't judge. We understand what they are trying to say or do and why. We see their behavior from their viewpoint. Many times people aren't right or wrong in an argument, they're just expressing different perspectives. Once we see something through their eyes, it will most certainly color what we are seeing with our own.

Give Me Limits

Children need and want limits, structure and consistency. This is especially necessary when they're young, but as much as they would argue against it, it's also true as young people mature. When people know the rules, what is expected of them, it's easier to live by those rules. Children are confused when something is okay when Mom is in a good mood, but not okay when she is upset. They can also feel insecure if they grow up in an environment where anything goes.

This insecurity was made clear to me when my niece, Valerie, was visiting us when she was about eight years old. Leigh was participating in *The Battle of the Network Stars* at Pepperdine University in Malibu, California. Valerie was watching the competitions with me. I was an indulgent aunt who adored my nieces and aimed to please. My nieces were well-behaved so I never felt like I was doing anything wrong by allowing them pretty much the run of things. On this particular occasion I was allowing Valerie to do just about anything she wanted to do. She had asked me for some money to get a soda, which I gladly gave her saying she could get anything she wanted. She suddenly looked up at me with a perplexed little face and asked, "Don't you love me?" I was shocked by her question.

"I adore you darling," I replied. "Why would you ask me such a question?"

"If you really loved me you wouldn't let me do anything I wanted to do. You would take better care of me and make sure I did the right thing."

My niece was begging for some structure and she was right. It's much easier to be a parent who lets his children do whatever they want to do. These parents never have any conflicts with their children. Everyone is happy until the kids wind up in juvenile court. "Misfortunes come in through a door that has been left open for them," Grandma's Maxim #78. It's more difficult to provide a structure for children and enforce it, to teach them right from wrong, to be a parent rather than to just be another kid.

I'm not suggesting that parents be the sole authority on children's rights and privileges. It works much better if children are involved in the process and you come to an agreement together about responsibilities and behavior. When the girls get into trouble, we ask them what they think the consequence should be. What would they do if they were the parents? In this way, they are never the victims. They know what behavior is expected of them and if they mess up, they take an active role in determining the outcome of the situation. They come up with some pretty good ideas. Many times a bad situation is made better because they learn something from it and end up acting responsibly.

The Power to Choose—Start Early,
Don't Wait for Prozac

When the girls were young, they would get a timeout if their behavior was inappropriate. The timeout ended when they were ready to change their behavior. They held all the power for the termination of their punishment. They were not victims. We stress that they have the power to change their behavior and their attitude. It's important to start young with this idea. Don't wait for Prozac.

Young or old, make sure that your child knows you love him unconditionally. You never stop loving him because he misbehaves. Brighton made me aware of this. Whenever I was angry with her behavior she would ask me, "Do you love me, Mommy?" I realized she needed to know the distinction between me being upset with her behavior and me loving her. I reassured her that my love for her was constant no matter what had occurred.

Think how much better we all would feel if we knew there were people who would love us unconditionally. Even if we messed up, they would still love us. They might get upset with us, but they would still love us. That's what parents are for, unconditional love. It makes a difference. Brighton has learned from my behavior. She is a secure young lady and if she makes a comment to me that she thinks may have hurt my feelings, she quickly follows it with, "I love you Mommy." Make sure your child knows that his behavior is the issue, not him.

Accentuate the Positive, It's so Small To Belittle

When one of our children misbehaves, Leigh and I stress that we know she's more loving or responsible than she has just demonstrated. We're careful not to sound patronizing. Grandma said, "Flattery is the food of fools," Maxim #58. Children catch on to empty flattery quickly and won't believe anything you don't mean. We believe our daughters are good people and, if they don't always act that way, we make sure they understand that we know this is not their usual type of behavior. Dear Grandma was wise when she often repeated to me, "Treat a man as he is and he will remain as he is. Treat a man as he can and should be and he will become as he can and should be," Maxim #2.

When Leigh was a child he never understood why adults would say to him, "You're too young to understand." He felt he understood quite well. He was young and didn't have the experience of the adults or their perspective of years, but he understood. He disliked being minimized. His pain was no less real because he was a child.

This condescension bothered him and he vowed to never treat children in the same manner. He would value their thoughts and respect their ideas. Yes, children need guidance, but their feelings are as important as any adult's.

Our children know that what they think and feel is important to us. We don't dismiss them as mere children who can't yet think or feel. I have never told them to run along and play so I can be with someone who matters. Many parents do this on a routine basis. I'm not suggesting that if your children are misbehaving or doing something annoying and you're trying to have a conversation with someone else that you should ignore their behavior. I wouldn't allow such conduct to continue, but I would act because the children's behavior is unacceptable in this situation, not because they are children.

Remember

Leigh's insight is important. He remembered how he had felt as a child and made sure he didn't make the same mistake with children that adults had made with him. Too often parents forget what it was like when they were young. They forget how they felt misunderstood, how they felt when they had a big crush on the guy who sat next to them in Algebra or how they felt when their mother was mad at them and they thought they hadn't done anything wrong. They forget why they wanted to stay out late with their friends. They forget how great it felt to ride a bike down the street with no hands. I have one word for all parents who forget: remember.

Leigh and I need to remind each other of this. It goes a long way in understanding and helping your children. When parents tell me they can't believe how much their daughter talks or texts on the phone, I ask them to remember what it was like when they were fourteen. Did they like to talk on the phone? When they are shocked at the clothes their child wears, I remind them of the bell-bottom pants and tie-dyed shirts that were a staple in our wardrobe. Many times parents affect a holier-than-thou attitude and, in reaction, become overly strict with their children. They expect their children to be perfect and forget what hell-raisers they were in their youth. It reminds me of the proselytizing television ministers who preach hell-fire and brimstone sermons and condemn anything but the straight and narrow path. Then you find out that these castigators are philanderers, embezzlers or worse. I'm a bit suspicious of parents who are severe and inflexible with their children. As Shakespeare wrote, "I think thou dost protest too much" comes to mind. Do they suspect their children because of their own guilty consciences?

This does not mean that it's okay for your child to do drugs or drop out of school because you were a complete misfit when you were in school, but it does help you put things in perspective and understand what they are experiencing. Remembering will aid you in discussing problems with your child and help them avoid some of the serious problems with which you have had to deal.

Your children have to learn certain things on their own, even if you try to protect them from any pitfalls. As parents we want to prevent our children from falling down. We try to catch them whenever we can. One has to realize that children do have to stumble and fall. It can save them from going off the deep end later if they learn how to deal with a problem when you're not there to cushion the blow. It's difficult when your children come to you in a panic because they didn't complete a homework assignment. You can help them occasionally, but if this occurs frequently it might be time for them to get a zero on the assignment. They will learn that if you let something go until the last minute, you can't always finish it on time. Grandma often quoted to me, "Give a man a fish and you feed him for a day; teach him how to fish and you feed him for a lifetime," Maxim #28.

Remember what it was like to be a child not only to understand your child's alien behavior or to protect him from the mistakes you made. Remember the joys you experienced and share those with your child. Stay up all night together and watch the sun rise. Make angels in the new fallen snow. Have a pillow fight. Watch one of those classic movies together that you adored when you were sixteen or listen to your favorite music from high school. They may not appreciate the Marx

Brothers, but they'll love the Beatles. Even if they don't, endure the rejection. They aren't you. Tastes change. Appreciate their individuality. Try learning about the music they like. Laugh and play and joke with your children: "A little nonsense now and then is relished by the best of men," Grandma's Maxim #45.

Who Said Being a Kid Was Easy?

"Your alarm has been ringing for five minutes. Are you deaf?"

"Get up right away. You'll be late again."

"Did you finish your homework? You always leave everything until the last minute. You'll probably flunk your test."

"You aren't going to wear that outfit to school are you? Your clothes are such a mess, just like your room. Don't expect me to clean it up, I'm not your servant."

"When was the last time you washed your hair? It looks terrible."

"Eat your breakfast. You'll get sick if you don't eat something healthy for a change. You never eat right."

And that is just the morning's conversation. You share a few warm words with your child to make him feel good about himself and ready to face the cold cruel world. No wonder children often prefer that cold cruel world to their warm loving home.

Reflect on what you say to your child. The scenario described above is all too common. If we could record ourselves and listen to all the comments we make to our children, the majority of us would be shocked. How could any of us have confidence or feel good about ourselves if we lived under such a barrage of criticism and orders? As parents we do it under the guise of trying to help our children be better people. We go off to our work and they go off to another onslaught of

165

demanding teachers, pressuring peers and dictating coaches. Who said being a kid was easy? It's amazing they live through it. Too often some don't.

As parents, we start early with our critiques and with the best of intentions. My friend, Janet, related the story of a day her young son, Eric, brought home his weekly school papers. He was a bright boy and did well in school. Janet sat with Eric and proceeded to look through his work. She passed through a number of his papers with A's, 100 per cent and excellent written clearly on each one saying, "Very good" or "Great job." She eventually came to one paper that had a B written on it. She reviewed it carefully.

"Eric, let's look at this paper. Do you see what you did wrong on number five?"

Her young son looked up at her and burst into tears.

"You always see what's wrong," he cried. "You never see what I do right."

Janet was mortified. She had the best intentions with her comments and actions. She wasn't upset with his grade or the fact he had incorrectly answered a problem. She had only wanted to help her son understand and learn from his mistake.

Janet had no idea how her actions were making her son feel. Even though she had complimented Eric on his other work, she had focused on the paper with the mistake. Luckily, for both Janet and her son, he expressed how he felt to her. Her lesson had been great and she never forgot it.

I've had my share of similar lessons. I sometimes wonder how I could be so stupid when I reflect on my behavior. All I can do is admit my failings to my child. "I'm sorry. You're right and I'm wrong." These are words that are not unfamiliar to my lips. I don't hesitate to utter them when I blunder. And blunder we will as parents, but we keep trying. My children know I'm not perfect and that I also make mistakes. I encourage them to tell me how they feel. Communication is the key. Never wonder if you should apologize to your child. "The greatest of faults is to be conscious of none," Grandma's Maxim #67. When you're wrong, admit it. It doesn't heal the wound completely — only changing your behavior can do that — but it starts the healing process.

The Most Important Time of All

Leigh and I love our garden. We add new plants and trees and enjoy the ones we planted in years past, which have become a gauge for the passage of time. We remember planting a tiny seedling and now look upon a towering tree. How did it grow so quickly? That new fertilizer must be working well. Then we realize it was actually five, ten or fifteen years ago that we planted it. Where did that time go?

The trees remind me that I must note the stages of growth carefully, enjoy each season, experience every moment or I will miss the whole process and our children will be grown.

Nature provides us with many valuable lessons. Our children are very much like the trees we plant. One day we will look at our children and wonder in amazement at the adults they have become. Where did it all go? It had to be just a few years ago when my college-graduate daughter was in nursery school. I don't know one parent who doesn't feel this way. Time goes quickly. Our children grow so fast. We must take the time to be with our children or they will be grown and, unlike that beautiful tree right there in the garden that you can still admire and even hug if you desire, our children could be far away from home studying, working, or raising their own families.

Leigh and I made the decision long ago that we would spend as much time as possible with our children and my happiest moments are when we are together. We've both given up time spent on our careers or individual pursuits, but we've gained so much in return. Grandma repeated the same point, "Things that matter most must never be at the mercy of things that matter least," Maxim #7. Love matters most. I'm convinced that's why we are here.

In so many families there are good intentions, but with everyone's busy schedules, times together as a family are too few. When families are together they often end up being on their computers or watching television and not sharing any thoughts or communicating in any way. I will not get started on the bane of technology, but I do have three words on the subject: turn it off. I can see how wonderful it is when our family is outside in the garden or if we go on a bike ride together or for a walk on the beach. I see how much we grow together, learn from one another, love one another. When I contrast that with the idea of us zoned out in front of a screen, rarely saying anything, there is no comparison about which is the healthier activity for our minds, bodies and souls.

If you must, schedule regular family time together and also one-on-one time, not just with your mate, but also with each of your children. Whatever it takes, do it. No excuses. It's a great idea to have a regular family day so no one schedules any outside activities during that time. Don't forget about having dinner together. There have been many studies which show that families who take this time together are happier and more successful. The children do better in school and everyone thrives.

Cooking is not my forte, but even if we don't have a meal together, I try to make sure we take time each day to enjoy each other.

I love family vacations. You don't have to actually leave your home if you don't want to or can't afford it. Take some time and just spend it together—even if it's in your own home. I adore our home and it would be a great vacation place, but sometimes it's easier to focus on one another with no distractions if you go somewhere away from your usual surroundings. There are many choices and price ranges from campground to world tour. Travel can be educational and inspirational, but I also find it beneficial for family bonding.

We just returned from a trip to Italy. Of course a trip to Italy is wonderful, but the best part about it was the time I had with Leigh and the girls. Caytlyn and I would walk down the streets of little Italian villages arm in arm chattering away like best friends. We don't often get a chance to do that at home. Brighton and I would lie in the grass together and make daisy chains while marveling at the clouds and the gorgeous light. We don't always take the time to notice these miracles when we are busy at home. Caytlyn and Brighton would stand side by side gazing at Michelangelo's *Pieta* for an hour, entranced by its beauty. When the girls are in school they are often involved in different activities with their own friends, but here they renew their lifelong bond. Leigh would hold us all tightly against the chilling wind in an enchanted Etruscan forest. We would listen to the talking trees and feel what they had to tell us. We return home enriched and inspired. Don't miss these special times together. "For all sad words of tongue or pen, the saddest are these: 'It might have been,'" Grandma's Maxim #21. Never regret time lost. Revel in time well spent.

Though Grandma would say, "Time waits for no man," Grandma's Maxim #89, time is malleable. It can contract and expand. Expand time to its fullest by savoring the moment. Don't let it pass away and realize too late that your children are grown and you have a bitter relationship with them or none at all. If you have decided to have children, be with those children. They aren't supposed to grow up without you. You have the sacred responsibility of being the caretaker of precious souls when you have children. If you can't live up to this responsibility, get a chinchilla.

~ If you want children, make sure you discuss this issue with your partner before you marry.

~ Keep your agreement unless you both agree to change it.

~ Parenthood isn't for selfish people or for wimps. Both of you must be ready to commit to it.

~ Avoid parenting pitfalls that can harm your relationship.

~ Share the responsibility of raising your children.

~ Don't always put the needs of your children before those of your mate.

~ Make time for each other.

~ You won't be good parents if you're not good mates.

~ Show your affection for each other in front of your children.

~ Bring your unique influences to your children, but present a united front.

~ Teach your children that a family is a team, you must all work together and help one another.

~ Listen to your children and understand before you try to be understood.

~ When you truly understand, you don't judge.

~ Children need and want limits, structure and consistency. Give those to them.

~ Include your children in the decisions you make. They will learn from their mistakes and realize that they're not victims. They have the power to change their behavior.

~ Make sure your children know your love for them is unconditional.

~ Accentuate your children's positive attributes.

~ Don't condescend to them because they're children.

~ Let your children know that what they think and feel is important.

~ Remember what it was like to be a child. It will give you great insight into your child's behavior.

~ Don't forget to laugh and play with your children.

~ Listen to what you say to your children.

~ Apologize and change your behavior when you are wrong.

~ Share yourself and your time with your children while they're still with you.

~ Be responsible caretakers of these precious souls.

Chapter Twelve

FRIENDS

Too often couples avoid anything outside their own intimate circle. They don't want to be with other people or expand their horizons, limiting their contact with the outside world. This is unfortunate because there are many people and experiences that can enhance your relationship with your mate. It's like breathing deeply: the more you have to breathe in, the more you can breathe out. You can give the breath of life to your relationship because you have more inside you to offer from your experiences with friends, just like your experiences with learning, working or traveling. You can both learn and grow by being with others and not just yourselves.

Silver and Gold

As a young girl I went to my share of summer camps. Many of the songs we learned at those camps were pretty hokey — remember "Found a Peanut?" — but there were some that still have meaning for me today. One of my favorites from Girl Scout camp was a round with the repeated ad infinitum lyrics, "Make new friends, but keep the old. One is silver and the other is gold." These words must have become ingrained in my brain because I still believe them. Friends are an important part of your life. Our friends have definitely enhanced Leigh's and my lives and relationship. We have kept our old friends and added many new ones. We are rich with our silver and gold.

Yesterday was a golden day. We had a wonderful gathering with many of our old friends, most of whom were in our wedding party many years ago. I treasure our long history together. These are the people who knew us when, who know us now and will probably know us forever. Sometimes a few months may go by between visits, but there is no awkwardness when we come back together. We fall in step with each other without missing a beat.

Our friends are an extraordinary group of people, all talented and exceptional in many different ways and when we get together we always find something fun to do. Sometimes we play baseball with all ages participating. When we were young the games were rather cutthroat, but even the most competitive of us has mellowed with age. We also play killer croquet, make funny videos, croon a few tunes, have great al fresco dinners on the balcony or just hang outside experiencing "another shitty day in paradise" as our friend, Casey, sardonically calls our perfect weather and garden. Our home has become the gathering place—our special reunion center for the extended family.

We continue to make new or silver friends primarily because of new people that come to our home for our discussion groups and through our work because we often go from project to project meeting new people. I welcome new friends and all the new ideas and experiences they bring. It's important to be open to new people in your lives. They may bring something important to you at the right time, or you may help them in a way that could change their lives. One of our newer acquaintances, Stanislas, is such a friend. He's an interesting fellow who has written a number of books on alchemy, a subject that especially fascinates Leigh. He is an excellent critic of Leigh's art because of his knowledge of symbolism. He understands and encourages Leigh's work. Leigh has introduced him to an organization with whom Stanislas now travels and lectures. We have stayed with him in Switzerland and Italy and helped him save his home in Malibu from being swept into the sea during the El Niño onslaught. In short, we have become dear friends and our lives are richer for it.

Enjoying Your Extended Family

Sometimes friends feel closer than family. When I was growing up, my family did not have many friends. For Leigh and me, extending our family circle came naturally. It helps that we know good people. Our friends are free of pretensions, jealousies, or any of the pettiness that sometimes seeps into some peoples' lives. Instead, there is much laughter and joy and support. Our girls benefit from the extra aunts or uncles who see them perform in plays or attend their birthday parties. Our friends have given the girls advice, support, and much love. When you choose your friends for all the right reasons, it's easy for those wonderful people to become part of your heart.

Leigh and I are relaxed hosts. We try to keep our home clean and tidy. I was raised on my Grandmother's Maxim #62, "A place for everything and everything in its place," but Leigh and I don't stress about having everything perfect for company. We tell people to help themselves to whatever they need. The refrigerator is open, they can take a towel for the beach, shower, spend the night, whatever: "Mi casa es su casa" is the rule. We love to have our friends here and they know this, but we don't wait on them. In fact, our friends often end up cooking for us. If we have something important to do, we do it. Our friends can join us or relax in the garden or go to the beach until we are finished. If they need time alone, we allow them their privacy. We have no expectations about how they must be with us. We not only do this with old friends with whom we are comfortable, but also with people we've only recently met.

Eventually everyone gets used to our open way and feels quite at home. People realize that they're being treated as a part of our family. At first some might be a bit hesitant to walk in the house and make a sandwich if they are hungry, but friends learn that it may be the only way they will get any food. Initially people might be a bit put off if I'm playing with the girls and don't seem entirely focused on them. When friends realize I'm listening to them, but I also need to be with the girls, they either join in the play or wait for a more private time.

The time I spent with my grandmother was my model for this behavior. I loved every moment and it just seemed right. Many times we would have discussions on her porch swing and spend our time together focused on each other, but just as often she would be rolling out noodles in the kitchen for her famous chicken soup and I'd go into the parlor and play something on the piano. After each piece she'd make a little comment or swing through the room with a smudge of flour on her nose to get a can of something from the pantry, dancing a few steps to the music. Sometimes I'd be engrossed in an interesting book and she'd sit next to me crocheting and we wouldn't say a word. We were completely comfortable around each other and didn't feel any specific behavior was necessary when we were together. We could be ourselves and do whatever was right at the time. This is why I have few formalities with friends. It seems like a richer relationship when you're each secure in the knowledge of the bond you have together and your behavior reflects this understanding.

To Have a Friend, Be One

"To have a friend, be one," Grandma's Maxim #3, is the most important maxim for friendship. Many people complain about being alone and miserable. They have no one to talk to, no friend to call. They have forgotten the basic tenet, "The way to be happy is to make others so," Grandma's Maxim #8. It's the only way to get out of your loneliness and misery. Get out there and help someone. Bring some joy into another's life and the joy will spill over on top of you. Grandma often said, "Love is a verb." You can choose to love by throwing off your pettiness, laziness, self-pity, whatever, and loving. Be kind and thoughtful to others. Remember, "The smallest act of kindness is never wasted," Grandma's Maxim #71. If you act acordingly, I guarantee you will be the most popular person in town.

Our friend, George, is an excellent example of this. He is joyful, loving, considerate. Everyone feels better just by being around George. Even when he has problems, he manages a smile and deals with them in his own quiet way. He's the perfect example of Grandma's Maxim #40, "A tea kettle can sing even though it's in hot water up to its nose." George has a plethora of friends. He's always the first name on anyone's list when there's a gathering. George has all these friends because he's the best friend anyone could want. Learn from George if you want to have friends.

Friendship - Not Too Much Work

A relative of mine once told me she had no time for friends, that they were too much work. Her attitude surprised me. She thinks she must take care of everyone and feels overwhelmed. I don't see my relationships with friends as work. I receive so much from my family of friends that anything I give is minuscule by comparison. It feels good to be a kind person and to genuinely care about people; it feels rotten to be rotten. I don't like how I feel if I'm upset with someone or hold a grudge. Grandma was wise when she said, "Hating people is like burning down your own house to get rid of a rat," Maxim #52. There may be rats out there, just don't let them in your house. Open your doors for the good guys. You will enrich many lives if you do, especially your own.

If you feel like it's too much work to have a friend and it's not enjoyable, you either have the wrong friend or the wrong concept of friendship. Doing something with or for a friend that feels good isn't work for me. There are times when a friend needs me and I may not feel like being there for them, but I still do whatever is necessary because we are friends. Very few of us look forward to getting out of bed at two o'clock in the morning to pick up a friend whose car has broken down, but of course we do it and he would do the same for us. If it happened all the time, it would seem more like an all-night taxi service than a friendship. We probably would not be so readily available and might suggest our friend get his car fixed or stop going out at two o'clock in the morning. It's true that friends don't take advantage of each other, but in a healthy friendship that idea isn't foremost in one's mind. If you're worrying about who did more for the other person you're in a competition and not a friendship. If you're worried about sharing your toys, then maybe you deserve to play alone.

We have had dear friends stay with us for extended periods of time while they were getting resettled after a break-up or during a move from another city. It can be true that "Guests and fish begin to smell after three days," Grandma's Maxim #38, but generally speaking, our friends blend in so well with our lives that we don't end up feeling this way.

The opposite is true when people get anxious about having everything perfect for their guests. I watched my "friends are too much work" relative nervously get ready for a dinner party when she was first married. When she started polishing the leaves of all the plants in the house, I thought she was getting a bit carried away. She worked so hard at trying to have the perfect dinner and got so stressed about everything that eventually she stopped having friends over to her house. She was right: having friends was not fun for her because it was too much work. Don't fall in this trap and deny yourself a wonderful part of life. It's much more important to enjoy your friends' company and feel relaxed than to try to present a picture of the perfect hostess. Who are you trying to impress? Be yourself and people will glow in the warmth of your hospitality. Your home will become their refuge and you will both look forward to seeing each other.

~ Enhance your relationship with your mate by having friends.

~ Remember the silver and the gold. Have both.

~ Choose your friends for all the right reasons.

~ Be relaxed hosts and have an extended family atmosphere in your home.

~ To have a friend, be one.

~ Be happy by making others happy.

~ Make love a verb.

~ Choose to love.

~ Friendship should not be too much work.

~ Don't deny yourself a wonderful part of life by trying too hard and not enjoying your friends.

Epilogue

NOW IS THE HOUR

I have talked a great deal about my grandmother in this book, but I haven't mentioned my grandfather. He died when I was two years old and the only things I knew about him I learned from a letter he wrote to me when I was born. I would often get my baby book down from the shelf in my grandmother's office, take out my grandfather's letter and read it aloud. My grandmother's eyes would tear up when she heard his words. This was unusual for my grandmother. She wasn't the crying kind. I had never seen her weep, so as a little girl I was intrigued by her behavior, not really sure what it meant. I thought that she must miss my grandfather and yet she rarely talked about him.

One day, when my grandmother and I were both much older, I brought down a box of old piano sheet music from the attic. The pages had turned yellow with age. I started to sing and play a song entitled "Now is the Hour." It was a pretty, sentimental tune. My grandmother had been sitting in the parlor knitting a scarf. Her hands were never idle. At the end of the song, she commented simply, "That was your grandfather's favorite song. He always played and sang it. I can see him sitting there now just as you are. It seems like yesterday and yet it was so long ago. I have had a full life with my family and friends, but I miss him."

A few weeks later, my grandmother passed away. I can see her sitting in her chair just as clearly as she saw her husband and it's been more than thirty years since that day. My grandfather's song still sounds in my ear. Now, truly, is the hour. Grandma would caution me about one poet's lament, "The song that I came to sing remains unsung. I have spent my days in stringing and unstringing my instrument," Maxim #32. Sing your song now. We must act now to make the changes we know we can make to have the good life we know is possible. Don't wait another hour, another minute. "We are here today and gone tomorrow– live today," Grandma's Maxim #10.

My Town

A few years ago I went back to the little town of Lodi, Wisconsin where I had grown up. I found I could go home again. It was a pleasure for me to visit all the special places where I had spent the first eighteen years of my life. I walked along the Lodi Creek and threw some kernels of corn to Susie the Duck and her latest brood of ducklings paddling along contentedly. Amazingly enough, she looked just like the Susie I remembered. I crossed the railroad tracks and looked to see if any wild asparagus was still growing there. Now that I no longer detested the taste of the stuff, I could not find a single stalk. I listened for the distant whistle of a train. I put a penny on the tracks, for old times sake, and made a note to come back and glimpse the latest rendition of smashed penny art. I stopped at the bakery for my favorite caramel doughnut. The tinkling bell sounded as I walked through the door announcing me to the workers in the back. I almost expected to see Mrs. Zimmerman or Trudy come up to the counter. I went up to the school and walked into the auditorium. A blaze of band and chorus concerts, sports events, dances and plays flashed through my mind.

The memory parade stopped on the community's production of Thornton Wilder's "Our Town." I had played Emily and her character rushed back to me. In the third act Emily dies, but decides she wants to go back to her life. She's warned against it by all the dead souls around her because it won't be what she expected. Nevertheless, Emily has to know for herself. She's warned to choose a day that wasn't important. Emily knows it has to be before she was married or had her child. She still wants a happy day, so Emily chooses her twelfth birthday. She relives the day, but it's not joyful for her. Emily sees that it all goes so quickly. She sees that the people she loves don't take the time to look at one another, to realize how important each moment of life is. Emily asks, "Do any human beings ever realize life while they live it? —Every, every minute?" It becomes clear to Emily that people don't understand much. She had not only lived a day in her life, she had watched herself live it and knew what was going to happen. Emily could see. We forget to see, to look at one another and truly see.

Roots

Lodi, my own "Our Town," was an extended family for me. I felt a special kinship with the people there. Many were old now, quite a few had passed away, some had moved on to other lives in different places. Had I ever really seen them? I decided to take a walk around the three-mile square that circled out of town and then back through the park to Grandma's red brick house on Main Street. I had many questions that I needed to ponder. Going outside and communing with nature always helped me get the answers I needed. Midway through my walk it started to rain, a soft gentle shower that seemed to aid my discussions with God and the universe instead of making me run for cover. I wondered why I'd been born in this tiny hamlet so far away and foreign to my present life. There didn't seem to be any connection between where I'd grown up and where I was now. The answer clearly came to me. "You were born here to establish strong roots. When you have strong roots you can be transplanted anywhere and you will flourish." I guess that was one of God's Maxims, a pretty good one too.

My roots have made me flourish and grow and I draw on their strength. It's often difficult to do the right thing, to see and make the changes that need to be made, but remember, "It is better to wear out than to rust out," Grandma's Maxim #42. Do the work that is necessary. Don't sit idly by and rust away unhappily to oblivion.

There is an old story about Olie who worked at the mill and brought his lunch to work with him every day. One day, Olie opened up his lunch box and bellowed, "I don't believe it! The same lunch! Every single day of my life I get the same lunch! I am so sick of this same disgusting lunch that I could scream!"

Olie's friend Sven looked over at him and inquired sympathetically, "Who packs your lunch?"

Olie looked back and replied, "I do."

How many times have we pulled an Olie? We complain and complain, but continue to pack the same lunch every day. It is time for a new menu. It's time to see.

I remember reading an article about the roots of the Chinese Bamboo Tree. When you plant this tree you'll see nothing for four years but a tiny shoot growing from the bulb. During the fifth year the tree suddenly grows to eighty feet tall. All the growth for the first four years is underground. You don't see it, but it's establishing its root system to sustain the eighty-foot tree that suddenly appears. Remember the Chinese Bamboo Tree. Don't give up even if you don't see any progress. It takes time to heal old wounds and set up new patterns. Start to establish your new roots today.

Whatever You Wish To Be, Be It

Grandma would often say, "If you wish to be a writer, write," Maxim #44. I wanted to do something to help other people and change their lives for the better. In one of those conversations I have with God and the universe, the message that came loud and clear was to write this book. I knew it was the right message, so I sat down and wrote it. I hope this book helps you achieve what you wish. Remember, whatever you wish to be, be it. Start being it today. Whatever you wish to do, do it. Start doing it today. Be it and do it every way, any way you can. Live your dream. "Life is what you make it," Grandma's Maxim #49. Make life good. Heck, make it exceptional!

I'll leave you with my very first maxim. Grandma would be proud. "If you want to be happy, love," Carla's Maxim #1. Practice loving every day. Have a loving relationship with your partner. Remember having a great relationship starts with you. "If you do not love yourself, who will?" Grandma's Maxim #50. Start slowly, but start today. Now is the hour. Go through your own looking glass and transform yourself. Know what is important. See and realize life while you live it. Develop the roots that can make you grow and live vitally. Be who you want to be. Love.

89 of Grandma's Maxims

1. Do unto others as you would have them do unto you.

2. Treat a man as he is and he will remain as he is. Treat a man as he can be and should be and he will become as he can and should be.

3. To have a friend, be one.

4. Do not put off until tomorrow what you can do today.

5. Live and let live.

6. Honesty is the best policy.

7. Things that matter most must never be at the mercy of things that matter least.

8. The way to be happy is to make others so.

9. There is no cosmetic for beauty like happiness.

10. We are here today and gone tomorrow–live today.

11. The proof is in the pudding.

12. Good to forgive, best to forget.

13. Never go to bed angry.

14. Things happen.

15. Laughter is the best medicine.

16. Manners are the grease that keeps the wheel of civilization turning.

17. The person who says it can't be done should not interrupt the person doing it.

18. Walk what you talk.

19. Absence makes the heart grow fonder.

20. You can't tell a book by its cover.

21. For all sad words of tongue or pen, the saddest are these: it might have been.

22. The family that plays together, stays together.

23. Be careful what you wish for, you might just get it.

24. What was hard to endure can be sweet to recall.

25. The first duty of love is to listen.

26. Out of sight, out of mind.

27. It's what's inside that counts.

28. Give a man a fish and you feed him for a day. Teach him how to fish and you feed him for a lifetime.

29. What's good for the goose is good for the gander.

30. Money can't buy happiness.

31. Use it or lose it.

32. The song that I came to sing remains unsung. I have spent my days on stringing and unstringing my instrument.

33. You must look into people as well as at them.

34. The journey of a thousand miles begins with one step.

35. The best thing parents can do for their children is to love one another.

36. Time tells all.

37. You can't always get what you want.

38. Guests and fish begin to smell after three days.

39. There are two tragedies in life. One is not to get your heart's desire. The other is to get it.

40. A tea kettle can sing even though it's in hot water up to its nose.

41. To each his own.

42. It is better to wear out than to rust out.

43. Variety is the spice of life.

44. If you wish to be a writer, write.

45. A little nonsense now and then is relished by the best of men.

46. The cup is half full, not half empty.

47. When there is marriage without love, there will be love without marriage.

48. Cleanliness is next to godliness.

49. Life is what you make it.

50. If you do not love yourself, who will?

51. See the doughnut, not the hole.

52. Hating people is like burning down your own house to get rid of a rat.

53. Rome was not built in a day.

54. What you are is god's gift to you. What you make of it is your gift to god.

55. If you expect nothing, you will never be disappointed.

56. If it's not broken, don't fix it.

57. Keep your eyes wide open before marriage and half shut after marriage.

58. Flattery is the food of fools.

59. Practice makes perfect.

60. A liar needs a good memory.

61. All for one and one for all.

62. A place for everything and everything in its place.

63. Easy come, easy go.

64. Character is what you are in the dark.

65. To everything there is a season, and a time to every purpose.

66. An obstacle is something you see when you take your eyes off the goal.

67. The greatest of faults is to be conscious of none.

68. Two wrongs do not make a right.

69. You catch more flies with a spoonful of honey than with twenty cases of vinegar.

70. A problem is a chance for you to do your best.

71. The smallest act of kindness is never wasted.

72. Wrinkles merely indicate where smiles have been.

73. When god gives you lemons, make lemonade.

74. At least when you are down you don't have to worry about falling.

75. You miss 100 % of the shots you never take.

76. If you can't say anything nice, don't say anything at all.

77. The biggest temptation is to settle for too little.

78. Misfortunes come in through a door that has been left open for them.

79. The purpose of life is a life of purpose.

80. Imitation is the sincerest form of flattery.

81. Every calling is great when greatly pursued.

82. A stitch in time saves nine.

83. Better late than never.

84. Where there's a will, there's a way.

85.   Necessity is the mother of invention.

86.   Seek and ye shall find.

87.   You cannot judge a man unless you have walked a mile in his shoes.

88.   Do not put the cart before the horse.

89.   Time waits for no man.

Biography

Carla McCloskey grew up in Lodi, Wisconsin. She studied in Spain and graduated from the University of Wisconsin before moving to Los Angeles, California. Carla was a teacher, theatre director, actor, musician and was selected to become an assistant director by the Producers Association. She was one of the first women in this position. She met her husband, Leigh J. McCloskey, her first day in "the business" on the television series, *Executive Suite*, in which Leigh was starring. Carla went on to be the assistant director on many films including *The Goodbye Girl, California Suite, Death Becomes Her, Point of No Return, Point Break, The 'Burbs, The Color of Night, Hook* and *Jurassic Park*. She worked with directors such as Steven Spielberg, Joe Dante, Robert Zemeckis, Richard Rush, John Badham, Herbert Ross, and Cher. She also worked on the television series *Amazing Stories, Babylon 5, Ally McBeal, Gilmore Girls* and *The Closer*. She began directing on *Gilmore Girls*.

Carla and Leigh live in Malibu, California. They have two daughters, Caytlyn and Brighton, and a wonderful menagerie of cats and dogs and various other animals. Leigh is an actor, artist and author. He has starred in many nighttime television series and films including the hit show *Dallas*. He has also starred in various theatrical films and daytime dramas including *Santa Barbara, General Hospital, Young and the Restless* and *Days of Our Lives*. Leigh continues acting as well as writing and publishing books (*Tarot ReVisioned, In the Splendor, Adam Reborn*

& *Eve Restored, The Codex Tor Series*), creating visionary works of art (*Hieroglyph of the Human Soul, Phoenix Arise* and the film, *Din of Celestial Birds*) and lecturing around the world. Leigh's art was featured on the Rolling Stones' *Bigger Bang Tour* and in Flying Lotus' CD and album art, *Cosmogramma*. Together with his daughter, Caytlyn, Leigh created Olandar, a clothing line that incorporates his archetypal images. Carla and Leigh have created the Olandar Foundation for Emerging Renaissance (OFFER.) Leigh's books, art and clothing can be seen on his websites, leighjmccloskey.com and olandar.com.

Carla has successfully counseled many friends and colleagues over the years and is often acknowledged as the therapists' therapist. She has written *Grandma Told Me So* to help others find and keep the best possible relationships in their lives.

Acknowledgements

I would like to thank Bill Wild for graciously publishing this book. He and his wife, Linda, have been dear friends for more than fifty years and are generous supporters of both Leigh's and my work. I would also like to thank Debbie Skinner and Christopher Clay for formatting the book and making the countless corrections.

And of course I thank my family—my mother, JoAnn V. Lichte, my daughters, Caytlyn and Brighton, and my husband, Leigh, for their support and most of all, their love.

Carla's Filmography

1976- *Executive Suite* (Series w/Leigh McCloskey, Mitch Ryan, Stephen Elliott, Madlyn Rhue, Ricardo Montalban)

1977- *The GoodBye Girl* (Feature produced by Ray Stark, written by Neil Simon, directed by Herbert Ross w/Richard Dreyfus-Best Actor Oscar and Marsha Mason)

1977- *The Other Side of the Mountain Part 2* (Feature w/Timothy Bottoms, Marilyn Hassett)

1977- *Loose Change* (Mini-Series w/Cristina Raines, Season Hubley, Theodore Bikel. June Lockhart, Stephen Macht, Ben Masters)

1977*- *Quincy* (Series w/Jack Klugman)

1977*- *Columbo* (Series w/Peter Falk)

1977- *The Incredible Hulk* (Series w/Bill Bixby, Lou Ferrigno)

1977*- *Telefon* (Feature directed by Don Siegel w/Charles Bronson, Lee Remick)

1978- *The Dark Secret of Harvest Home* (Mini-Series directed by Leo Penn w/Bette Davis, David Ackroyd, Rosanna Arquette, Rene Auberjonois, Norman Lloyd, Joanna Miles, Michael O'Keefe, Donald Pleasence)

1978- *California Suite* (Feature produced by Ray Stark, written by Neil Simon, directed by Herbert Ross w/Bill Cosby, Richard Pryor, Michael Caine, Maggie Smith, Walter Matthau, Elaine May, Jane Fonda, Alan Alda)

1979*- *The Main Event* (Feature w/Barbra Streisand, Ryan O'Neil)

1979*- *Ravagers* (Feature w/Richard Harris, Ernest Borgnine)

1979- *A Force of One* (Feature w/Chuck Norris and Jennifer O'Neill)

1979*- *Just You and Me, Kid* (Feature w/George Burns, Brooke Shields, Burl Ives, Ray Bolger)

1980- *Roughnecks* (TV Movie w/Steve Forrest,Vera Miles, Harry Morgan, Wilford Brimley)

1980- *Seizure:The Story of Kathy Morris* (TV Movie w/Leonard Nimoy and Penelope Milford)

1983*- *The Fall Guy* (Series w/Lee Majors)

1984-1988*- *Murder She Wrote* (Series w/Angela Lansbury)

1985*- *Code Name: Foxfire* (Series w/Joanna Cassidy, John McCook, Sheryl Lee Ralph)

1985*- *Misfits of Science* (Series w/Dean Paul Martin, Courteney Cox, Kevin Peter Hall)

1985-1986- *Alfred Hitchcock Presents* (Series produced by Christopher Crowe)

1985-1987- *Amazing Stories* (Steven Spielberg Series w/amazing directors and amazing actors)

1986*- *Jumpin' Jack Flash* (Feature w/Whoopie Goldberg)

1987*- *MacGyver* (Series w/Richard Dean Anderson)

1987*- *Charles in Charge* (Series w/Scott Baio)

1987*- *Out of this World* (Series w/Donna Pescow, Burt Reynolds, Doug McClure)

1987*- *Nothing Is Easy* (Series w/Dee Wallace-Stone)

1987*- *Three O'Clock High* (Feature directed by Phil Joanou)

1988-1989*- *Simon & Simon* (Series w/Gerald McRaney, Jameson Parker)

1989- *The 'Burbs* (Feature directed by Joe Dante w/Tom Hanks, Carrie Fisher, Bruce Dern, Henry Gibson, Cory Feldman)

1989*- *Quantum Leap* (Series w/Scott Bakula, Dean Stockwell)

1990*- *Point Break* (Feature directed by Kathryn Bigelow w/Patick Swayze, Keanu Reeves, Gary Busey)

1990-91- *Hook* (Feature directed by Steven Spielberg w/Robin Williams, Dustin Hoffman, Julia Roberts, Bob Hoskins, Maggie Smith, Phil Collins, Gwyneth Paltrow, David Crosby, Glenn Close)

1991*- *Dream On* (Series w/Brian Benben)

1991*- *Harry and the Hendersons* (Series w/Bruce Davison, Kevin Peter Hall)

1991*- *Mr. Baseball* (Feature directed by Fred Schepisi w/Tom Selleck, Ken Takakura)

1992*- *Death Becomes Her* (Feature directed by Robert Zemeckis w/ Meryl Streep, Goldie Hawn, Bruce Willis)

1992- *Point of No Return* (Feature directed by John Badham w/Bridget Fonda, Gabriel Byrne, Anne Bancroft, Harvey Keitel, Dermot Mulroney)

1992- *Jurassic Park* (Feature directed by Steven Spielberg w/Sam Neill, Laura Dern, Jeff Goldblum, Richard Attenborough, Samuel L. Jackson)

1993- *Color of Night* (Feature directed by Richard Rush w/Bruce Willis, Reuben Blades)

1994*- *Baywatch* (Series w/David Hasselhoff)

1995- *Lightning* (TV Movie directed by Joe Dante w/Brian Keith)

1996*- *Pacific Blue* (Series w/Mario Lopez)

1996*- *Moloney* (Series w/Peter Strauss)

1996*- *Multiplicity* (Feature directed by Harold Ramis w/Michael Keaton)

1996- *If These Walls Could Talk* (TV Movie produced by Demi Moore, directed by and starring Cher w/Anne Heche, Jada Pinkett Smith, Eileen Brennan, Craig T. Nelson, Rita Wilson, Diana Scarwid)

1997-98- *Babylon 5* (Series created by J. Michael Straczynski w/ Bruce Boxleitner)

1998*- *Felicity* (Series created by J.J. Abrams w/Keri Russell and Scott Speedman)

1999- *Crusade* (Series created by J. Michael Straczynski w/Gary Cole and Tracy Scoggins)

1999-2000- *Ally McBeal* (Series created by David E. Kelley w/ Calista Flockhart, Jane Krakowski, Portia de Rossi, Lucy Liu)

2000-2005- *The Gilmore Girls* (Series created by Amy Sherman-Palladino w/Lauren Graham, Alexis Bledel, Melissa McCarthy, Kelly Bishop, Edward Herrmann)

2005-2006- *Los Simuladores* (Spanish Series filmed in Madrid, Spain)

2007- *Pretty Handsome* (TV Movie directed by Ryan Murphy w/ Joseph Fiennes, Carrie-Anne Moss, Blythe Danner, Robert Wagner)

2006-2009- *The Closer* (Series w/Kyra Sedgewick)

*Did not work on complete series or film

Leigh's Filmography

1975- *Phyllis* (Series w/Cloris Leachman) -*Donald Ralston*

1975- *Secrets of Isis* (Afternoon Special) -*Bill Cady*

1975- *Streets of San Francisco* (Series w/Michael Douglas and Karl Malden) -*Gil*

1976- *Rich Man, Poor Man* (Miniseries w/Nick Nolte, Peter Strauss, Susan Blakely) -*Billy Abbot*

1976- *Medical Center* (Series w/Theodore Bikel and Chad Everett) -*Mihail Zankov*

1976- *Bert D'Angelo/Superstar* (Series w/Paul Sorvino) -*Elliot Becker*

1976/77- *Executive Suite* (Pilot & Series Regular) -*Brian Walling*

1976- *Blind Sunday* (Afternoon Special) -*Jeff*

1976- *Dawn: Portrait of a Teenage Runaway* (Movie of the Week) -*Alexander Duvall*

1977- *Alexander: The Other Side of Dawn* (Movie of the Week) -*Alexander Duvall*

1977- *Hawaii 5-0* (Series w/Jack Lord) -*Ted Bonner*

1978- *The Bermuda Depths* (Movie of the Week w/Burl Ives, Connie Selleca, Carl Weathers) -*Magnus Dems*

1978- *Doctors Private Lives* (Movie of the Week) -*Kenny Weiss*

1979- *Buck Rogers* (Series w/Dorothy Stratton) -*Jalor Davin*

1979- *The Paper Chase* (Series w/John Houseman) -*Paul Chandler*

1979- *Married the First Year* (Series Regular) -*Billy Baker*

1980- *Inferno* (Feature directed by Dario Argento) -*Mark Elliot*

1980-82, 1985, 1988- *Dallas* (Series Regular)-*Mitchell Cooper*

1981- *Hart to Hart* (Series w/Florence Henderson, Robert Wagner, Stephanie Powers) -*Vernon Custobur*

1982- *The Love Boat-Greek Isles* (Series) -*Ralph Berrows*

1983- *Hearts in Armor* (Feature) -*Rinaldo*

1983- *Mike Hammer* (Series w/Stacey Keach) -*Carl Pentington*

1983- *First Edition* (Series)

1983- *Hotel* (Series) -*Hank Miller*

1983- *Fantasy Island* (Series w/Ricardo Montalban)-*Paul Spencer*

1983- *The Fall Guy* (Series w/Lee Majors) -*Web Covington, Jr.*

1983- *Velvet* (TV Movie) -*James Barstow*

1984- *Finders of Lost Loves* (Series) -*Travis Burke*

1984- *Partners in Crime* (Series w/Loni Anderson and Linda Carter) -*Kasey Quinn*

1985- *Hotel* (Series) -*Lou Valentine*

1985- *Just One of the Guys* (Feature) -*Kevin*

1985- *Fraternity Vacation* (Feature w/Tim Robbins) -*Charles "Chas' Lawlor*

1985- *Hollywood Beat* (Series) -*Eddie Cooper*

Filmography

1985- *Black's Magic* (Series) *-Paul Thompson*

1985- *The Love Boat* (Series) *-Chip Reynolds*

1985- *Murder She Wrote* (Series w/Angela Landsbury) *-Todd Amberson*

1986- *The Love Boat-Hong Kong* (Series w/Eddie Albert) *-Peter Adams*

1986- *Hamburger the Motion Picture* (Feature) *-Russell Procope*

1986- *Crazy Like a Fox* (Series w/Jack Warden) *-Bob Buyers*

1986- *Hotel* (Series) *-Joel Shubert*

1986- *Dirty Laundry* (Feature) *-Jay*

1986- *We've Got It Maid* (Series) *-Barry*

1986- *Cameron's Closet* (Feature) *-Pete Groom*

1987- *Love, American Style* (Series) *-Bob Turner*

1987- *Love, American Style* (Series) *-Peter David*

1987- *Jake & the Fatman* (Series w/William Conrad) *-Glen Latamer*

1988- *Sonny Spoon* (Series) *-Dick Darling*

1988- *Double Revenge* (Feature) *-Mick Taylor*

1988- *Santa Barbara* (Series Regular) *-Dr. Zach Kelton*

1988- *Lucky Stiff* (Feature directed by Anthony Perkins w/Donna Dixon) *-Eric West*

1988- *The Bronx Zoo* (Series) *-Richard*

1989-91- *Santa Barbara* (Series Regular) *-Ethan Asher*

1990- *Shades of LA* (Series) -*Dr. Ernest Lindstrom*

1992- *Jake & the Fatman* (Series) -*Hank Goldman*

1992- *Life Goes On* (Series) -*Philip Jorgens*

1992- *General Hospital* (Series Regular) -*Dr. Michael Baranski*

1993- *Raven* (Series w/Lee Majors) -*Randall*

1993- *Trouble Shooters:Trapped Beneath the Earth* (Movie of the Week w/Kris Kristofferson) -*Frank Matther*

1993-96- *General Hospital* (Series Regular) -*Damian Smith*

1994- *Accidental Meeting* (Movie of the Week w/Linda Grey and Linda Purl) -*Richard*

1994- *Chicago Hope* (Series) -*Soap Doctor*

1996- *Terror in the Shadows* (Movie of the Week w/Genie Francis) -*Alex Williams*

1997-98- *The Young and the Restless* (Series Regular) -*Kurt Costner*

1997- *The Nancy Travis Show* (Series)

1997- *Star Trek Voyager* (Series) -*Tieran*

1997- *Babylon 5* (Series) -*Thomas*

1997- *Almost Perfect* (Series) -*Tommy*

1998- *Deep Space 9* (Series) -*Joran Belar*

1998- *3rd Rock From the Sun* (Series w/John Lithgow) -*Matthew*

1999- *I Might Even Love You* (Feature) -*Hank Price*

1999- *Jag* (Series) *-Dan Landertor*

1999- *Beverly Hills 90210* (Series) *-Bigelow*

1999-2000- *One Life to Live* (Series Regular) *-Drake Farraday*

2001- *Brutally Normal* (Series) *-Corey*

2001- *The Seagull* Odyssey Theatre Los Angeles *-Trigorin*

2003-2004 - *Gone But Not Forgotten* (TV Movie w/ Brooke Shields and Scott Glenn) *-Detective Barrow*

2009- *An Elaborate Plan* (Short) *-Donald Cavanaugh*

2011- *Bones* (Series) *-Lee Coleman*

2013-2014 - *The Young and the Restless* (Series Recurring) *-Dr. Kurt Costner*

2014- *Before Your Eyes* (Short) *-Ben*

Leigh as Artist and Author

I wrote *Grandma Told Me So* before Leigh created *The Hieroglyph of the Human Soul* in his upstairs studio or wrote his books including *Tarot Revisioned* and the *Codex Tor* series.

The following pages include some of the images from Leigh's work that I have not discussed in this book, but are too important not to share with you. Enjoy!

Views of Leigh's studio,
The Hieroglyph of the Human Soul

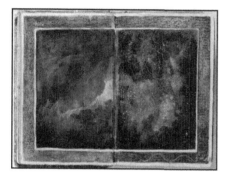

Images revealing the beauty, artistry and mystery of Leigh's remarkable illuminated **Codex Tor** *Books. The three volumes consist of over five hundred images that chronicle the creative adventure and vision of Leigh's work as a visual philosopher.*

One of Leigh's **Code**
images used for the c
of Flying Lotus' al
Cosmogra

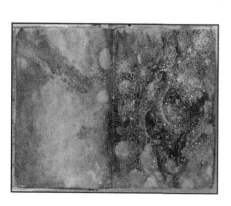

Justice from Leigh's Tarot Revisioned

The Lovers from Leigh's Tarot Revisioned

Phoenix Arise

Universe as Organism #5

*An image from Leigh's Grimoire (French word for book of Spells and Magick) which was originally created for his friend, the director E.Elias Merhige (*also see: **Din of Celestial Birds**) and his film **Shadow of the Vampire** with Willam Defore and John Malkovitch. The Grimoire was not in the final edit of the film and through a rather magical course of creative connectivity ended up being used by the Rolling Stones on their Bigger Bang Tour.*

Universe as Organism #1

211

Olandar Press LTD
Olandar Foundation for Emerging Renaissance
(OFFER)

4900 Pine Cone Circle • Middleton, WI 53562
Ordering Information: *Contact Amy Meicher @ 608-831-1222*
Or www.olandar.com • www.leighmccloskey.com

- Search Leigh McCloskey on the internet to see more of his works and associations. Use keywords with his name like "art," "Rolling Stones," "Grimoire" and "Flying Lotus," and "Creation."

- Go to www.youtube.com and search Leigh McCloskey to see videos of some of his works.

Olandar Press Tarot ReVisioned products that are available for purchase.

212

*Codex Tor Illuminated books, Adam Reborn & Eve Restored,
Phoenix Arise Mandala cards and many more works of
Leigh's art available for purchase.*

Leigh J. McCloskey
Author, Artist, Actor and
Visual Philosopher

www.leighmclosky.com

facebook - *Leigh J. McCloskey and
Olandar Foundation for Emerging
Renaissance for more insight into
Leigh and his works.*

CPSIA information can be obtained
at www.ICGtesting.com
Printed in the USA
LVOW05*0413110116

469205LV00002B/2/P